AND THE DEPRESSION, 1861-1924

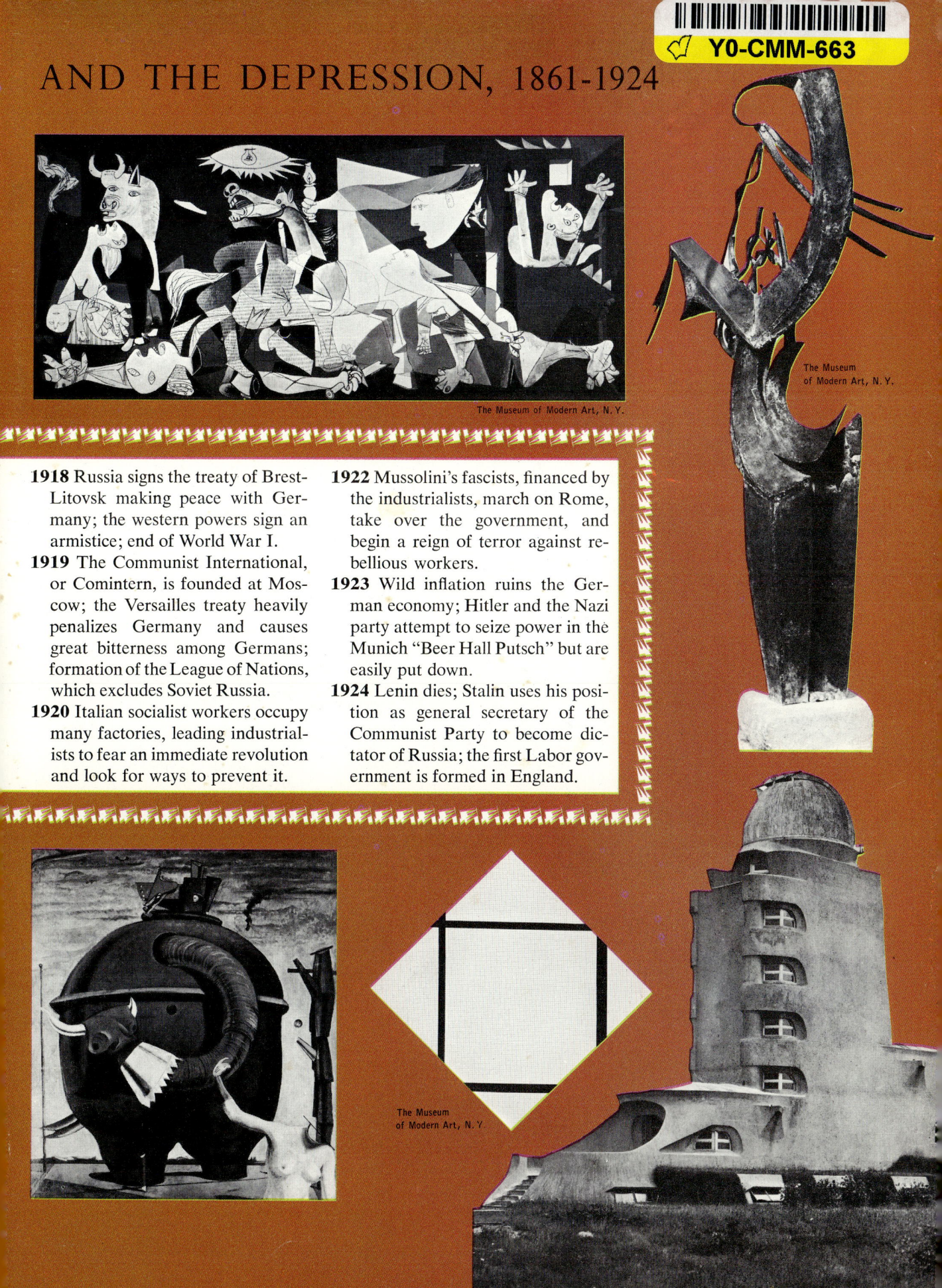

1918 Russia signs the treaty of Brest-Litovsk making peace with Germany; the western powers sign an armistice; end of World War I.

1919 The Communist International, or Comintern, is founded at Moscow; the Versailles treaty heavily penalizes Germany and causes great bitterness among Germans; formation of the League of Nations, which excludes Soviet Russia.

1920 Italian socialist workers occupy many factories, leading industrialists to fear an immediate revolution and look for ways to prevent it.

1922 Mussolini's fascists, financed by the industrialists, march on Rome, take over the government, and begin a reign of terror against rebellious workers.

1923 Wild inflation ruins the German economy; Hitler and the Nazi party attempt to seize power in the Munich "Beer Hall Putsch" but are easily put down.

1924 Lenin dies; Stalin uses his position as general secretary of the Communist Party to become dictator of Russia; the first Labor government is formed in England.

HISTORY OF

Editor	Irwin Shapiro
Associate Editor	Jonathan Bartlett
Consultant	Albert Fried, *Department of History, Queens College, New York*
Contributors	Anne Howard Bailey
	John Bowman
	Ormonde de Kay, Jr.
	Edith Firoozi
	Albert Fried
	Johanna Johnston
	Ira N. Klein
	Willis Lindquist
	Edna Ritchie
	Seymour Reit
	James L. Steffensen

IMPORTANT EVENTS – TOTALITARIANISM

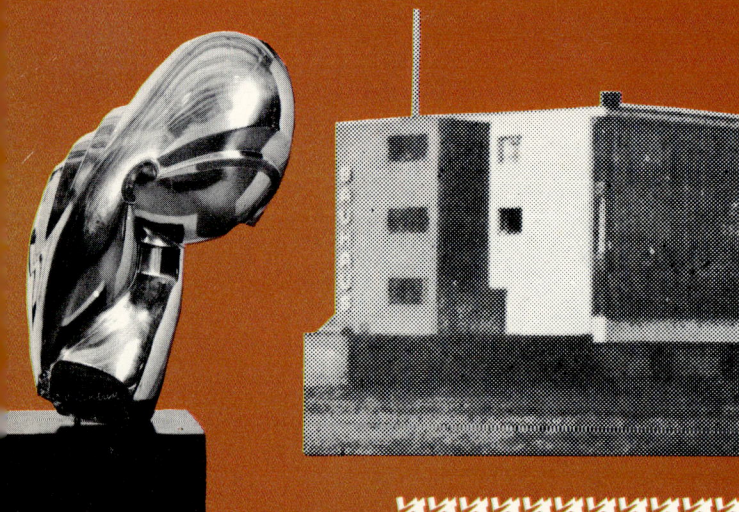

1861 Tsar Alexander II signs a decree abolishing serfdom in Russia.
1881 Terrorists assassinate Alexander; his successor, Alexander III, is more autocratic.
1903 Russian Marxists split into two groups, the Mensheviks, and the Bolsheviks led by Lenin.
1904 Russia and Japan go to war.
1905 Russia is defeated by Japan; widespread discontent flares into open revolt against the tsar after petitioners are cut down on "Bloody Sunday"; the revolt is suppressed with difficulty.
1914 World War I begins.
1917 Heavy war losses and famine lead to a new revolt in Russia; the tsar abdicates and a provisional government takes over which is later led by Kerensky; Lenin, Trotsky, and the Bolsheviks gain the support of the soviets and lead them to take over from the provisional government; Soviet Russia begins peace talks with Germany.
1918-1920 Civil war rages in Soviet Russia; the anti-Bolshevik forces are finally defeated by the Red Army under Trotsky.

The Museum of Modern Art, N.Y.

The Museum of Moder

VOLUME XIV

THE UNIVERSAL

THE WORLD

TOTALITARIANISM AND THE GREAT DEPRESSION

by Edna Ritchie

GOLDEN PRESS NEW YORK

CONTENTS

Blood on the Snow 1855-1905 — 1127
The tyranny of the tsars brings bloodshed, and revolutionary movements grow.

Workingmen of all Countries, Unite! 1848-1900 — 1131
The ideas of Marx and Engels become the guide of the Russian revolutionaries.

The 1905 Revolution 1905 — 1135
Lenin becomes leader of the Bolsheviks, but the revolt is repressed.

Rasputin and War 1914-1917 — 1143
Russia enters World War I. Rasputin gains influence with the tsarina and is killed.

The March Revolution 1917 — 1147
The people overthrow the tsar. Kerensky and Lenin become prominent.

The November Revolution 1917 — 1148
The soviets under Bolshevik leadership overthrow Kerensky's government.

Peace — and Civil War 1917-1924 — 1152
Soviet Russia makes peace with Germany. The Red Army wins the civil war.

Stalin Succeeds Lenin 1924-1939 — 1153
Stalin takes power and builds industry at a cost of countless lives.

Fascism and Mussolini 1918-1936 — 1160
Mussolini becomes dictator and conquers Ethiopia.

© COPYRIGHT 1966 BY WESTERN PUBLISHING COMPANY, INC., AND LIBRAIRIE HACHETTE. ALL RIGHTS RESERVED INCLUDING THE RIGHT OF REPRODUCTION IN WHOLE OR IN PART IN ANY FORM. DESIGNED AND PRODUCED BY ARTISTS AND WRITERS PRESS, INC. PRINTED IN THE U.S.A. BY WESTERN PRINTING AND LITHOGRAPHING COMPANY. PUBLISHED BY GOLDEN PRESS, INC., NEW YORK.

Revolution in a Beer Hall 1923-1924 1164
Hitler attempts to seize power with his Brown Shirts but fails and is imprisoned.

"My Struggle" 1167
Hitler writes Mein Kampf, *his plan for taking power in Germany and the world.*

Fire in the Reichstag 1923-1933 1168
Hitler becomes chancellor and the Nazis seize power.

Germany Under The Nazis 1933-1939 1174

Dictatorship and a Civil War 1926-1939 1179
Franco overthrows the Spanish republic. Dictatorship spreads.

The Meaning of Totalitarianism 1183

Panic in Wall Street 1929-1932 1184
The crash marks the start of the depression in the United States.

The New Deal 1933 1188
Roosevelt becomes President and enacts measures to deal with the crisis.

A Changing Nation 1934-1936 1192
The New Deal bolsters national morale, and trade unions grow.

The Election of 1936 1936 1195

Roosevelt Battles the Court 1937-1939 1200
Roosevelt tries unsuccessfully to enlarge the Supreme Court.

"On the Dole" 1918-1936 1203
The depression strikes England. A Labor government is elected but has little effect.

Democratic But Divided 1926-1938 1206
Fascists attempt to take over in France, but are defeated by the Popular Front.

Totalitarianism Versus Democracy 1210

TOTALITARIANISM AND THE GREAT DEPRESSION

Blood on the Snow
1855-1905

It was a Sunday in January of 1905, and snow lay on the ground and rooftops of St. Petersburg, the capital of Russia. Although winters were cold in this northern city, and it seemed like a day to sit indoors before a warm fire, many people were hurrying through the streets. About 200,000 men, women, and children gathered in huge crowds, their breath making puffs of vapor in the frosty air. Soon they formed processions and began marching across the hard-packed snow. As they tramped along in ragged lines, they sang the national anthem, "God Save the Tsar." Many of them carried icons—religious paintings—or pictures of their ruler, Tsar Nicholas II, whom they called "the Little Father."

The processions started from various points of the city, but they all moved toward the same place—the tsar's Winter Palace. And yet this was no celebration, no festival, no holiday. The marchers were not parading for pleasure. The city's metal workers had staged a four-day strike for better working conditions, such as the eight-hour day. To teach them a hard lesson, their employers had then shut down the shops, completely cutting off their pay. Now the workers were going to the palace to ask the help of the tsar. At the head of one of their processions walked Father Gapon, the priest who was their leader. He would present petitions to the Little Father.

And so the people marched under the heavy winter sky, singing their country's song, holding up the icons of their saints and the pictures of their ruler. But the Little Father was suspicious of his children. Afraid that they might rise up against him, he had called out his soldiers and left St. Petersburg. As the processions drew closer to the center of the city, where the palace stood, the soldiers blocked off the streets. Suddenly, obeying their officers' orders, the soldiers raised their rifles and fired into the crowd. The marchers fled, crying out with rage and fear. But the soldiers fired again and again, and there was blood on the snow. No one ever knew exactly how many of the marchers were killed, but the number was between five hundred and a thousand, and that day became known as "Bloody Sunday."

"THE DARK PEOPLE"

It was not the first time in recent years that there had been blood on the snow. Russia was a land of tyranny, and the tsars did not hesitate to use violence against their own people. As usual, violence was answered with violence. The people had no vote and no part in the government. If they wanted a change in the way they were ruled, they, too, had to use violence.

ON "BLOODY SUNDAY" IN ST. PETERSBURG, MOUNTED COSSACKS ATTACKED AND CUT DOWN DELEGATIONS OF WORKERS TRYING TO PRESENT A PETITION TO THE TSAR.

TSAR ALEXANDER II

1127

And there was great need for a change. Until about the middle of the nineteenth century, more than forty million Russians were serfs. Other European nations had done away with serfdom, but in Russia it went on as it had in the Middle Ages. The serfs were little better than slaves. Although they were farmers, they could not own land. They could not work where they pleased, or live where they pleased, or even marry whom they pleased. They had no rights in the courts of law. They were given no education, and few of them could read or write. Living in the darkness of ignorance and poverty, they were often called the "Dark People."

When Alexander II became tsar in 1855, he realized that the serfs were becoming more and more dissatisfied. He said, "It is better to abolish serfdom from above than wait until it begins to abolish itself from below." He realized that if he did not free the serfs himself, they might revolt against their masters, overthrow the government, and free themselves. In 1861—two years before Abraham Lincoln signed the Emancipation Proclamation, which freed the slaves in the United States—Alexander II ordered serfdom in Russia "forever abolished."

Alexander II also ordered other reforms. He set up local government councils, called *zemstvos,* in the farming areas. Peasants called up to the army no longer had to serve for as long as twenty-five years; they now served six years in the regular army and nine in the reserve. Even so, life was hard for the peasants. They were allowed to buy or rent land from the aristocrats, but the high payments and taxes made it impossible for them to live decently. They still did not have all the rights that had been given to other Russians. Furthermore, there was no freedom of speech or of the press for anyone, let alone for the peasants.

In spite of his reforms, Alexander II had no intention of giving up his power as tsar. He mercilessly smashed a rebellion in Poland. In Russia itself, he had many weapons to use against those who opposed him. He had the police and the army. He had the Cossacks, the skillful horsemen and savage fighters who were organized into special cavalry units. He could execute people, imprison them, or send them out of the country into exile. With these weapons, he put down uprisings of peasants and demonstrations by students of the universities. He put down ideas as well, for his ministers controlled education and censored newspapers and magazines.

And yet he could not stop people from thinking. During his reign, writers such as Tolstoy, Turgenev, and Dostoyevsky were writing books that would become famous throughout the world. Musicians like Borodin, Moussorgsky, Rimsky-Korsakov, and Tchaikovsky were composing music. Scientists like Mendeleyev and Metchnikoff were at work. And, most important of all to Alexander II, there were men who were thinking and writing about politics and government.

Many of these men had been exiled to other lands, but their books and ideas were smuggled into Russia. A new political movement sprang up. It was called the narodnik movement, taking its name from the Russian word *narod,* which means "the people." The narodniks were not satisfied with reforms. They wanted to replace the tsar with a completely new government that would give land to the peasants and freedom to all Russians. This, of course, meant revolution, and the revolution would have to come from the people, particularly the peasants. But when the narodniks tried to carry their message to the peasants, they met with little success. Most of the narodniks were well educated, and the uneducated peasants were suspicious of them. Besides, there were no more than a few thousand narodniks in all, and it was an easy matter for the police to track down and arrest any of them.

DYNAMITE AND BOMBS

Some of the tsar's opponents decided that there was only one thing to do. They must fight violence with violence. If the tsar would not let them speak out, they would speak to him in the language of terror and assassination, with pistols and dynamite and bombs. Meeting secretly in small bands, these terrorists plotted and planned —and acted. They tried to assassinate Alexander II so many times that once he cried out, "Why do they hunt me down like a wild beast?"

Alexander II began to plan another reform, a new constitution that would limit his powers a little. Then, on March 13, 1881, he was driving in his carriage in St. Petersburg. A bomb exploded, injuring some of his guards. When he got down from the carriage, a second bomb landed at his feet—and this time it was the blood

Blood on the Snow

RUSSIAN TERRORISTS MADE MANY ATTEMPTS TO ASSASSINATE ALEXANDER II, AND FINALLY SUCCEEDED.

of a tsar that was spattered on the snow. He was carried to the Winter Palace, where he soon died, surrounded by the royal family.

Except for a small number of revolutionists, all Russia was shocked by the assassination of Alexander II. Even the people who wanted reforms and changes in the government were horrified; they felt that bloodshed would not solve Russia's problems. The peasants still had a great respect for their rulers, and they mourned the death of their Little Father.

Alexander III, the big, strong, bearded man who now became tsar, dropped the plan for a new constitution. Rather than limit the monarchy, he would strengthen it. He believed that anything resembling democracy was like a disease that had to be stamped out. There would be no reforms or changes while he reigned. His police tirelessly hunted down the revolutionists. His ministers tightened their control of education and the press. He persecuted minority groups, especially the Jews. Jews were not allowed to own land, and only a very small percentage were allowed to enter the schools and universities. The government was openly anti-Semitic, and the police helped to stir up pogroms, the organized massacres of Jews that took place in various parts of the country. Alexander III looked to the past, and not to the future, and a kind of darkness fell over Russia.

And yet, no matter how much Alexander III hated change, there was change. Russia was still mainly a farming country, but industry was growing rapidly. As industry grew, so did the number of industrial workers, and they formed a class that was new in Russia. Nor could all the police and soldiers and Cossacks keep people from thinking. Even in prison, even in exile, there were Russians who were thinking of politics and government. And, more and more, they were turning to new political ideas—ideas that would some day shake not only Russia but the entire world.

TSAR ALEXANDER II DIED FROM THE WOUNDS HE RECEIVED IN THE BOMBING.

Workingmen of All Countries, Unite!

1848-1900

The ideas that attracted these Russians came mostly from a man named Karl Marx. Marx was born in Germany in 1818, the son of Jewish parents who had become converted to Christianity. He began the study of law, but soon dropped it to study philosophy. After receiving his degree of Doctor of Philosophy from the University of Jena, he became the editor of a newspaper. When the German government ordered the paper to stop publication, Marx moved to Brussels. He returned to Germany to take part in the unsuccessful revolution of 1848, but by 1850 he had settled in London, where he would live until his death in 1883.

Meanwhile, in 1844, Marx had met Friedrich Engels. The two men thought very much alike, and from that time on they worked closely together, studying, discussing, writing, each helping the other. Engels, too, was a German. He came from a wealthy family, and he carried on his father's business, even though he hated business and had no use for businessmen. For many years he supported Marx, who had little money and few opportunities to earn any.

Both men believed in socialism. They were not the first socialists, nor were they the only ones in Europe at that time. Other men were also looking to socialism as a way to solve the problems of the world. For a great change had taken place in Europe in the nineteenth century. Before, Europe had been agricultural; now, industry was growing at a furious rate. Before, work had been done by hand; now, many kinds of work were being done by machine. Before, Europe's system of society had been feudalism; now, it was capitalism. People were flocking to the cities; machines were roaring; smoke was pouring out over the once green countryside. Kings and aristocrats were no longer as important as they had been in the past. The owners of factories and large businesses were the real rulers. As industry grew, these owners became rich. But most people, who owned nothing and had to work for others to make a living, were poor. It seemed as if the rich were continually getting richer, while the poor were getting poorer. Many families found it so hard to make a living that women and even small children were forced to take jobs in factories and mines.

Socialism seemed to offer a way out. If all the people owned the means of production—the factories, mines, mills, railroads, and so on—and shared in the profits, there would be no rich and no poor. But the socialists were not very definite about how this could be accomplished. Besides, they could not agree on the reasons for what was happening. Socialism seemed no more than an ideal—and Marx felt it should be more than that.

Day after day, Marx went through the foggy streets of London to the reading room of the British Museum. There he spent long hours studying books, pamphlets, reports, statistics. He believed that, by using the methods of philosophy he had learned in Germany, he could make socialism scientific. Working with Engels, he developed new ideas of socialism. In time, this kind

KARL MARX IN 1863

Workingmen of all Countries, Unite!

MARX AND ENGELS COLLABORATED IN WRITING *THE COMMUNIST MANIFESTO*.

of socialism would be called communism, and the principles laid down by Marx would be called Marxism.

Marx and Engels were not content with writing and talking; they believed in action as well. They wanted new political parties, organizations of workingmen which would help bring about socialism. In 1847, they helped form such an organization, the Communist League. They wrote a statement of what the League stood for, the *Communist Manifesto,* and in it they summed up their own beliefs.

All history, said Marx and Engels, is the history of class struggles. By this they meant that the people of all societies were divided into classes—roughly, the class that rules, and the class that is ruled; the class that owns the wealth, and the class that creates it. These two classes were opposed to each other and fought for power. Sometimes the ruling class was pushed out, and the society was changed. At other times, both classes were ruined in the fight.

In the societies of the past, there had been a complicated system of classes. But in modern times, society was split into two classes. On one side was the industrial middle class—the millionaires who owned the giant industries. On the other side was the working class.

The middle class had already brought about a great revolution. It had accomplished wonders and had changed the world. It had opened the entire globe to trade, had put to use all kinds of inventions, and had developed all kinds of industries. In doing this, the middle class had made itself rich. But the workers remained poor.

Why? Why hadn't the workers become rich, too? The reason, Marx and Engels said, was in the way modern society produced the goods it needed. People no longer made everything they needed, with families raising their own food, building their own houses, making their own clothes, and all the rest. Instead, they made certain things for sale, and bought others. All goods were bought and sold. But nobody would pay money for things that were worthless. All goods, therefore, were worth a certain price; they had value. And they had value because of the work that had gone into them. Iron ore, for example, was worth little while it lay in the ground. But when it had been dug up and made into iron, it had considerable value.

The workers, who did the actual work that gave goods value, got back only a small part of the value, in the form of wages. The rest went to the owners of the means of production, the middle class, in the form of profits. The workers were paid barely enough to live on. They had all they could do to keep going from day to day. Meanwhile, the middle class was gathering in more and more money. Indeed, the rich were getting richer, while the poor were getting poorer.

Furthermore, under capitalism, nothing in modern society was planned. Sometimes the manufacturers produced too much, and unsold goods piled up in warehouses. Then business was bad and many people were thrown out of work. These periods of hard times were becoming more and more frequent, and each was worse than the one before.

Surely there were many things wrong with a society that could not furnish its people with the necessities of life. Could nothing be done to right these wrongs? Through unions and other such organizations, workers could win better conditions for themselves. But reforms were not enough. They could not solve the basic problems of capitalism. The workers must take over the government and all the means of production and run them for the benefit of all the people. And, since the middle class would never willingly give up its power, that meant revolution.

Even after the workers had successfully made a revolution, the middle class would still be strong. To keep the middle class from gaining power again, a dictatorship of the working class would be set up. In time, however, all people would be workers. No man would be able to grow rich on the work of other men. The result, for the first time in history, would be a society without different classes. There would then be no need for a dictatorship. As Marx and Engels put it, the state would "wither away." With the use of machinery and modern methods of farming and manufacturing, enough goods would be produced for all. Each person would do the kind of work he was best suited for, and each would receive everything he needed to live well. Another way of putting it was: "From each according to his abilities, to each according to his need."

But wouldn't a revolution turn everything topsy-turvy? Not really, said Marx and Engels. It was the middle class that had actually turned everything topsy-turvy. The people of the middle class not only owned the means of production, but with their wealth they controlled men and ideas. They controlled the government, the courts of law, the police, the army, the press. Even religion was controlled by the middle class. It was just another way of fooling people; it promised them a reward in heaven if they changed

FRIEDRICH ENGELS IN 1864

Workingmen of all Countries, Unite!

nothing on earth. Under capitalism, there could be no real freedom for the majority of men. Only under communism could poverty be abolished; only under communism could mankind be free.

And Marx and Engels ended the *Communist Manifesto* with a call to action that rang out like the sound of a bugle on a battlefield. The workers, they said, "have nothing to lose but their chains. They have a world to win. Workingmen of all countries, unite!"

There was more to Marxism than this, of course. Marx explained his ideas in greater detail in three huge volumes entitled *Capital*. He and Engels both wrote numerous works on many topics. There was hardly a field of thought they did not touch on. History, economics, philosophy, politics—Marx and Engels wrote about them all.

Marxism taught that revolutions of the working class would take place first in the most advanced countries—those that were highly industrialized—rather than in backward countries like Russia. Surprisingly, many Russian thinkers began to believe that Marxism might be the best guide to political action in Russia. And yet, perhaps it was not so surprising, after all. There was no freedom in Russia. Everything was tightly controlled by the tsar's government. The narodniks had failed to bring about a change; the terrorists had failed. Marxism seemed to explain what was happening in the world and to show the way to the future.

And so the Russians who wanted change studied Marxism. Some of them—those who had been sent to Siberia or exiled to foreign lands as a punishment for their political beliefs—had plenty of time to study. Political prisoners in Siberia were not actually imprisoned. They were allowed to live in small, lonely settlements. It was the cold, barren land itself, the vast distance from the rest of Russia, that was their prison. They could read and study and write, and Siberia became their school of Marxism. The Russians who were exiled to foreign lands could read books forbidden at home, and have discussions with foreign Marxists. They wrote books and pamphlets themselves, and published newspapers and magazines, which were smuggled into Russia. These publications did not reach a great number of people. But they did reach the intellectuals—the educated and thinking people. The intellectuals would become the leaders of a movement that would end the rule of the tsars forever.

WHEN FAMINE STRUCK, HUNGRY RUSSIANS WAITED IN LINE FOR FOOD.

RUSSIAN PRISONERS BEGINNING THE LONG JOURNEY TO SIBERIA

The 1905 Revolution

SOME DAY there would be no tsars, but there was little sign of that during the last years of the nineteenth century. Alexander III still held Russia in a firm grip. And when he died in 1894, his son Nicholas II came to the throne. Nicholas was twenty-six years old. He was a handsome young man, and a few months after his father's death he was married to a German princess. They were in love, and it looked as though Nicholas would be a popular ruler.

But his reign began badly. In 1896, a great crowd gathered on a field in Moscow to celebrate his coronation as tsar. It was the custom to hand out little presents, such as handkerchiefs and cups, at these celebrations. Afraid that there might not be enough for everyone, the crowd surged forward. When mounted police tried to hold back the crowd, men, women, and children were pushed into ditches, and two thousand persons were killed. To make it even worse, that same night the tsar and the tsarina, his wife, danced at a ball held at the French embassy. People grumbled that the tsarina was a foreigner who had no feeling for Russians, and the tsar was not much better.

Nor did the people like the tsar's reply to a message of congratulation from the officials of a town near Moscow. The officials said that they hoped "the rights of individuals and public institutions will be firmly safeguarded." Nicholas answered that he would support the principle of absolute rule just as firmly "as it was preserved by my unforgettable great father."

It was plain that under Nicholas the Russians could expect no greater freedom than they had had under Alexander III. There would be no civil liberties, no better treatment of the peasants and of minority groups. There would still be

ON THE FOLLOWING PAGES, THE CORONATION OF NICHOLAS II AND ALEXANDRA IN USPENSKY CATHEDRAL IN MOSCOW

1135

the soldiers, the Cossacks, and the secret police to enforce the tsar's orders, and his spies would be everywhere. And, as time went on, the Russians realized that, unlike his father, Nicholas was a weak man. He was not the ruler the country needed.

In 1901, out of what remained of the narodnik party, a new party grew—the Social Revolutionaries. They were mildly socialistic, and interested in getting land for the peasants. They believed in democracy. But within the party was a terrorist group called the "Fighting Organization." Even more strange, this group was headed by a secret agent of the police, a man named Azev. He turned over many members of his group to the police; at the same time, he plotted the death of many people in the government. Later, when the truth about him became known, it was impossible to say on which side he had really been. At any rate, the "Fighting Organization" assassinated hundreds of officials, including governors, ministers, police chiefs, and grand dukes.

Through his secret agents, the tsar learned that another party had also been formed—the Russian Social-Democratic Workers' party. Its members were Marxists, and to avoid the Russian police, they met in Brussels, Belgium, in 1903. The Belgian police forced them to move the meeting to London. There the members continued to argue, for they could not agree on the organization of their party. One group, led by Vladimir Ilyich Lenin, wanted a tightly controlled party, with membership open only to professional revolutionists. The second group wanted a looser kind of party, with membership open to anyone who would support its policies. Lenin's group won, and it became known as the Bolsheviks, or "those of the majority." The other group became known as the Mensheviks, or "those of the minority." Both groups wanted revolution; they differed on the methods of bringing it about.

Neither the Mensheviks nor the Bolsheviks seemed to be much of a threat to the tsar; there were so few of them. Besides, Nicholas had other things on his mind. He wanted more territory to rule, territory that might bring in riches. The Russians pushed on into Manchuria, and then into Korea, where they came into conflict with the Japanese. Negotiations went on between Russia and Japan, but the Russians were not really interested in reaching a settlement. In February of 1904, the Japanese attacked Russian ships at Port Arthur and Chemulpo. The tsar and his advisers were rather pleased that the Japanese had struck. They had no objection to war. There was nothing like a nice little war to stir up patriotism and make people forget their troubles.

The Russo-Japanese War turned out to be anything but a nice little war. The Russians made one mistake after another, and disaster followed disaster. As for the Japanese, they were winning battles, but it was costing them more than they could afford in men and money. When the president of the United States, Theodore Roosevelt, offered to serve as peace-maker, both sides were glad to accept. In August of 1905, after about a year and a half of fighting, they signed a peace treaty at Portsmouth, New Hampshire.

For Tsar Nicholas, it was already too late. His people had hated the war and were deeply discontented with the government. Already, in January of that same year, the workers of St. Petersburg had marched to the palace behind Father Gapon. That was the day called "Bloody Sun-

LENIN LED THE BOLSHEVIKS, THE MOST MILITANT OF THE RUSSIAN SOCIALISTS.

ABOVE: A CARTOON OF ROOSEVELT MAKING PEACE BETWEEN THE RUSSIANS AND THE JAPANESE. RIGHT: THE RUSSIAN GENERAL GRIPPENBERG PULLED BACK HIS TROOPS AS THE JAPANESE ATTACKED.

A JAPANESE PRINT OF WARSHIPS BOMBARDING PORT ARTHUR

SAILORS ON THE *POTEMKIN* MUTINIED WHEN ORDERED TO SHOOT THEIR COMRADES.

day," when the tsar's soldiers had fired on the crowd. After "Bloody Sunday," Father Gapon wrote to the tsar: "The innocent blood of workers, their wives and children, lies forever between thee, O soul destroyer, and the Russian people." Not only workers, but peasants and professional people, wanted a change. There were strikes, riots, assassinations. Sailors on the battleship *Potemkin* mutinied.

In October, a strike of railroad workers started in Moscow. Spreading to other parts of the country, it set off strikes in many industries. A general strike shut down St. Petersburg, the Russian capital. Here the workers were joined by professional people—by doctors, lawyers, teachers, bankers, and ballet dancers. Even businessmen closed down their shops and factories, some of them giving strike pay to their workers. Huge

1140

THEIR REVOLT HELPED INSPIRE RESISTANCE TO THE TSAR THROUGHOUT RUSSIA.

crowds gathered in the streets, carrying red banners—the banners of revolution. All the inhabitants of the city seemed to have decided, at one time, to show that they were dissatisfied with the government.

During October, the factory workers of St. Petersburg elected delegates and set up a central council to run the strike. The Russian word for council is *soviet*—a word that would someday become known to the entire world. During October, too, still another political party was formed in Russia, the Constitutional Democratic party. The Constitutional Democrats were more often called the Cadets, a name suggested by their initials. They were in favor of a democratic government with a parliament like Britain's.

With the country in turmoil, the tsar and his ministers were forced to take action to save them-

The 1905 Revolution

selves. They issued an order giving civil liberties to the people. They also agreed to set up a *Duma,* a kind of parliament, with elected representatives. This satisfied the Cadets, who stopped supporting the strikes, and the government began to win back control of the country.

Even so, the turmoil was not yet ended. The Social Democrats, most of whom were in exile, had sent a brilliant young man named Leon Trotsky to St. Petersburg. He had helped to organize the St. Petersburg Soviet, and for a while had been its head. Now Lenin, too, returned to Russia, where he worked with the Moscow Soviet. Lenin and Trotsky tried to turn the revolt into a Marxist revolution of workers. There was some street fighting in Moscow, in which about a thousand persons were killed, but the government was more and more in control of the situation. Trotsky and a number of other Social Democrats were arrested, and Lenin fled from the country.

The Revolution of 1905 was over.

What had it accomplished? What had the people gained? It soon became clear that they had not won true democracy. The tsar's promise of civil rights meant little. The Duma had no real power; that was still in the hands of the tsar. What he allowed one day, he forbade the next. Revolutionaries were still hunted down. There were still pogroms against the Jews. But the government did put through some reforms that made it easier for the peasants to get land, and they were given the same rights as other Russians. Russia was not democratic, but it had taken the first step toward democracy—a small, fumbling step, but still a step.

During the years that immediately followed the 1905 Revolution, industry grew. The condition of the workers improved somewhat, although a number of miners were shot down in a disturbance at the Lena goldfields in 1912. Perhaps Russia might have gone the full distance to democracy, if it had not been for the outbreak of war—war, and the character of the tsar and the tsarina, and a strange peasant named Grigori Yefimovich Rasputin.

AT LEFT, WITH HAND UPRAISED, IS TROTSKY, AT FAR RIGHT IS STALIN, AS THEY APPEARED IN THE EARLY REVOLUTIONARY YEARS.

Rasputin and War
1914-1917

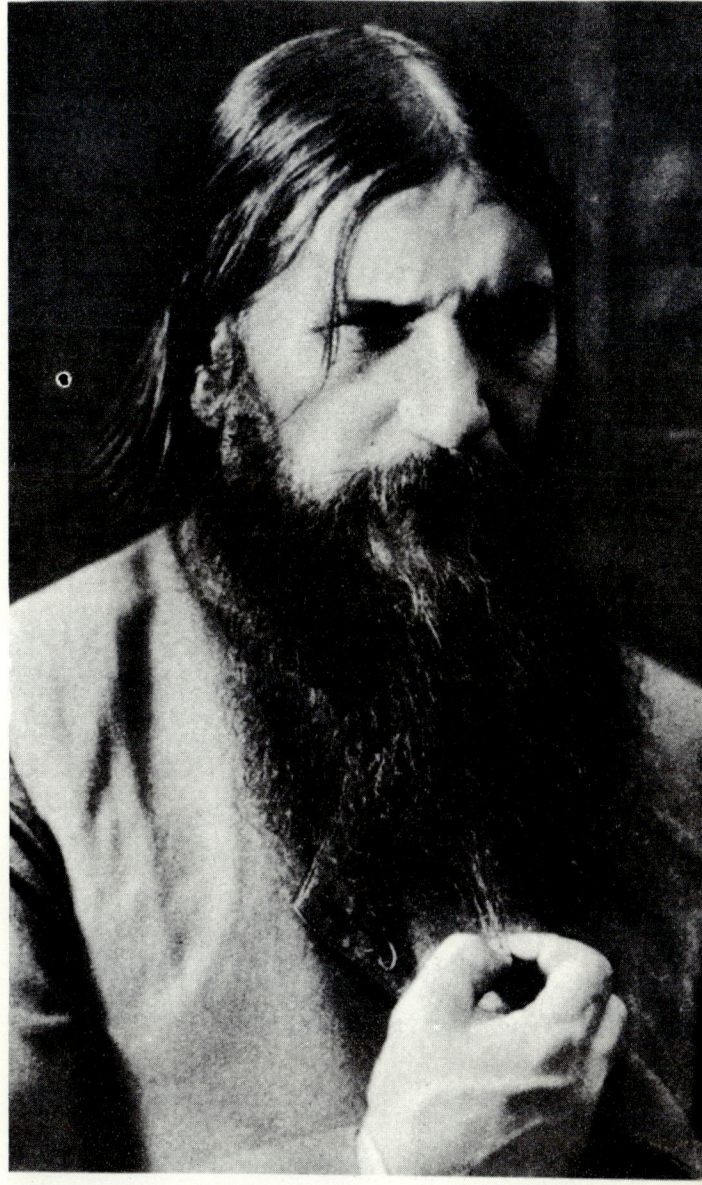

RASPUTIN

The Tsarina Alexandra was a religious woman. That was why she was immediately interested in Rasputin when he was introduced to her in 1905. Rasputin was neither a priest nor a monk. He was a *starets,* or Holy Man. There were a number of such Holy Men in Russia at that time. They left their homes and families to wander about the country, living on charity and devoting themselves to religion. Often people came to them, hoping to hear words of wisdom and advice on how to conduct their lives.

The tsarina, too, felt the need of someone to give her advice and words of wisdom. She was troubled by the problems of the tsar; she kept urging him not to give up any of his power. And then there was her fifteen-month-old son. He was the tsarevitch, the prince who would some day be tsar—if he lived. For he suffered from hemophilia, a hereditary disease that prevented his blood from clotting properly. Even a slight wound might cause him to bleed to death.

THE HOLY MAN

Rasputin became a frequent visitor to the palace. It turned out that he had a strange ability to soothe and comfort the tsarevitch and make him forget his pain. Some people said that he hypnotized the boy. At any rate, Alexandra came to believe that her son's life depended on Rasputin, and her faith in him grew from day to day.

With his long beard, and his long hair that reached to his shoulders, Rasputin did indeed look like a Holy Man. But the life he led had little to do with holiness. He had an enormous appetite for food and drink. It was no secret around the palace that he spent many a night in wild, drunken parties, staggering home early in the morning. When Alexandra was told this, she refused to listen. Nothing could shake her faith in Rasputin. He had saved the life of her son. He was a Holy Man who could do no wrong.

Many Russians were worried about Rasputin's influence on the tsarina. Then, in August of 1914, World War I began. France, an ally of Russia, had been attacked by Germany, and called for the Russians to strike at Germany in the east. The tsar agreed to enter the war, and a great wave of patriotism rolled over Russia. The people forgot Rasputin. They forgot their dissatisfaction with the government and the tsar, and rallied behind him to fight for their country. They hung out the flag, they prayed, they fell to their knees

1143

Rasputin and War

The people might have been less enthusiastic if they had known the condition of the army. Russia was not prepared for war. The Russian soldier was a good fighting man, but his leaders knew little of modern warfare, and many of them were dishonest. Supply was a problem; there were not enough arms and ammunition. Within a year, Russia lost Poland, Lithuania, and a large part of the Ukraine and White Russia. Millions of men were killed or captured. The government turned on the Jews and mercilessly hunted down anyone suspected of spying, but that won no battles.

And now Nicholas showed his weakness and Alexandra her strength. More and more, the tsar acted on her advice—and she was guided by Rasputin. In September of 1916, Nicholas himself took over the supreme command of the army. The actual rule of the country was left in the hands of Alexandra and Rasputin. Rasputin was not bashful about using his authority. He dismissed and replaced ministers and many other important officials, and controlled the church as well.

None of this helped to change the course of the war. In 1916, as the terrible Russian winter came on, men were still dying at the front by the thousands. Soldiers who managed to survive began to desert from the defeated army. At home, they found everyone confused, hopeless—and hungry, for food was becoming scarce. Meanwhile, the tsarina was writing to the tsar: "Be the Emperor . . . crush them all under you. . . . We have been placed by God on the throne, and we must keep it firm and give it over to our son untouched."

TSAR NICHOLAS AND TSARINA ALEXANDRA

and sang "God Save the Tsar." The Duma supported the war. The name of the capital was changed from St. Petersburg, which sounded too German, to Petrograd, a Russian form of the name. The country was united, and the tsar and tsarina seemed filled with new energy.

MURDER OF RASPUTIN

But even the aristocrats, even the people who believed in monarchy, were deeply troubled by what was happening to their country. Speeches were made in the Duma bitterly criticizing the tsarina and Rasputin. To save the country and himself, the tsar must remove Rasputin from a position of authority.

The tsar did nothing, and Prince Felix Yusupof decided to act for him. Prince Yusupof was a wealthy aristocrat and the husband of Princess Irina, the tsar's niece. In the last months of

1144

1916, he plotted with a group of monarchists to kill Rasputin. As part of their plan, Yusupof invited Rasputin to his house. There is some dispute as to what argument Yusupof used to persuade Rasputin to accept the invitation, but in any case he did accept. Around midnight of December 29, Prince Yusupof took the towering Holy Man to a room in the cellar of his house. There, on a table, were poisoned cakes and poisoned wine. In a room above sat the other plotters, waiting for news of Rasputin's death. While they waited, they played a record of "Yankee Doodle" on the phonograph.

They had a long wait. Rasputin ate a few of the poisoned cakes and drank a number of glasses of the poisoned wine, but by two-thirty in the morning he was still alive. Yusupof went upstairs to consult the other conspirators, came back down, shot Rasputin, and left him lying on the floor. When Yusupof returned a little later, he was horrified to see Rasputin move. Rasputin rose, followed him up the stairs and, roaring, broke through a locked door into the courtyard. One of the conspirators shot him again and kicked him after he fell, and Yusupof beat him with a steel rod. Rasputin was then thrown into the icy water of the Neva River, where his body was found on January 1.

RESTLESSNESS AND REVOLT

And so, at last, the strange career of Rasputin had come to an end. His murderers were punished only lightly for their crime. They were aristocrats; besides, too many people sympathized with them. There were few Russians who were not glad to hear the news of Rasputin's death—but nothing was changed. The tsar and tsarina ruled as they had before. High government officials and army officers discussed all sorts of plots to get rid of the tsar, but nothing was done. And something had to be done, for every day the people were growing more restless, more dissatisfied, more ready for revolution.

Members of the tsar's own family tried to tell him this and urged him to take action before it was too late. He refused to listen to their advice. During January of 1917, the temperature in Petrograd dropped to forty below zero, and it seemed as if all Russia were frozen in hopeless-

THE PLOTTERS SHOT RASPUTIN WHEN THEIR POISONED WINE FAILED TO KILL HIM.

ness and despair. And then, in March, Russia exploded into action. The explosion was set off, not by plotting aristocrats and army generals, not by bands of terrorists or revolutionists, but by the people themselves. And it came about because they wanted bread.

1145

The March Revolution
1917

It BEGAN in the Russian capital, in the city which had been called St. Petersburg and was now called Petrograd. Bread had been rationed, and on March 8, 1917, crowds of women and boys formed into long lines at the bakeries to get their share. Russians were used to waiting in line, and usually they were patient. But on this day they were hungry. Besides, they were tired of the war, tired of the tsar, tired of living without hope. When they learned that there was no bread to be had, they lost their patience. They suspected that the bread was being held back to force a rise in prices. The women and boys rioted, and the police were called out. Workers who had been on strike joined the rioters. They swarmed into the streets, marching and chanting, "We want bread! We want bread! We want bread!"

In the days that followed, more and more workers left their jobs and went on strike. There were more riots. The police lost control, and mobs roamed the city, calling for bread, peace, and freedom. They looted shops, tore down the emblems of the tsar from buildings, broke into police stations, and let prisoners loose from the jails. Soldiers were ordered to stop the mobs and to shoot if necessary. But many of the soldiers were raw recruits who came from families of peasants or workers. They, too, wanted bread and peace and freedom. They refused to fire on the mobs; instead, they joined them in battling the police. Even the Cossacks, those fierce fighters who had never hesitated to beat down the people—even they mingled with the crowds. Scenes like this were repeated in city after city; all Russia wanted peace, bread, and freedom.

With comparatively little bloodshed—less than 1,500 persons were killed—the people had

THE REVOLUTION OF 1917 BEGAN WITH FIGHTING IN PETROGRAD.

brought about a revolution. The workers of Petrograd set up a soviet which took over part of the Tauride Palace for its offices. In another part of the same palace, an emergency committee of the Duma met. Soldiers refused to take orders from the tsar, and without the army he had no power. On March 15, Nicholas agreed to give up the throne and turn it over to his brother, the Grand Duke Michael. Michael refused to accept it, and at last Russia had no tsar. With the support of the Petrograd soviet, the Duma set up a provisional, or temporary, government. It was to call an election of a Constituent Assembly, or parliament. Meanwhile, the tsar and his family were placed under arrest.

The next few months were months of excitement, confusion, and uncertainty. Both the provisional government and the Petrograd soviet issued orders, and often it was hard to tell which was ruling the country. The Russians had overthrown the tsar—but what were they to do now? Should they try to build a democracy modeled on that of England? Or should they try a mild form of socialism? Or should they go on with the revolution until workers and peasants governed according to the ideas of Karl Marx? And there were other questions to be decided as well. Should they continue the war or make a separate peace with Germany? And how could they get the country back on its feet? How could they get the factories working and the trains running? Above all, how could they get enough food for the people?

The Russians had made a revolution without any real leadership, but now the professional revolutionists quickly became active. So did members of other parties. Bolsheviks, Mensheviks, Social Revolutionaries, Cadets, moderate liberals, and men of every shade of opinion appealed to the people for support. They made speeches and put out newspapers. They issued slogans and announcements. Meetings were held on street corners, in factories, and in buildings once open only to the aristocrats. Soldiers and sailors came streaming back from the front to join the crowds arguing politics.

Out of all the turmoil, two men rose to prominence. One was Alexander Kerensky, who was at first minister of justice, then war minister, and finally head of the provisional government. A moderate socialist, he was a skillful orator, young and full of energy. The other man was Lenin.

The November Revolution
1917

LENIN'S REAL name was Vladimir Ilyich Ulianov. Like most Russian revolutionaries, he had taken another name to protect himself from the police. He looked like anything but a leader of men; someone once said he looked more like a small-town grocer. He was short, stocky, and bald, and wore a small beard. His clothes were shabby, and his pants were usually too long. He was not a great orator. But he had a gift for simplifying and explaining complicated questions, which made him an effective speaker before crowds.

Lenin was born in 1870, the son of a schoolteacher who became an official in the school system. The family was fairly well off, and no different from thousands of other Russian families. Then Lenin's older brother, Alexander, went off to study in the Russian capital. Young Alexander became involved in a plot to assassinate the tsar, and was hanged with four other students. Lenin was seventeen at the time, and he, too, became a revolutionist. He studied law, completing a four-year course in one year. He practiced law for a while, but soon became a full-time revolutionist. He was arrested, sent to prison for fourteen months, and to Siberia for three years. After this, with his wife, Krupskaya, he spent most of his time in exile. They went from one European country to another, and were often very poor. Wherever they were, Lenin never stopped studying, writing, and working for the revolution. In 1917 he was in Switzerland, impatient to get back to Russia where so much was happening. He was in touch with the Bolsheviks there, and sent them instructions, but that was not the same as being on the spot. Because of the war, however, it seemed impossible for him to travel across Europe.

It was the German government that made his return to Russia possible. The Germans were anxious to stir up a Bolshevik revolution in Russia, in the hope that Russia would then drop out of the war. Lenin and a small group of other revolutionaries were carried in a sealed German train to Petrograd, where they arrived on April 16. A large crowd, carrying banners and accompanied by a band, greeted Lenin at the Finland Station. He addressed the crowd, but, as always, he was not interested in playing the hero. He was interested in one thing, and only one thing. He wanted to change the revolution that had already taken place into a revolution of workers, and to set up a government based on the teachings of Karl Marx. He immediately began meeting with the Bolshevik leaders and outlining his plans.

They were bold plans, and they startled many of the other Bolsheviks. According to Lenin, the provisional government would never establish socialism and must be overthrown. "All power to the soviets!" he said. These councils of workers and soldiers, once they were led by the Bolsheviks, would bring about the revolution. To the people, Lenin offered the slogan of "Peace, bread, land." This was what the people wanted above everything else. The workers would support a revolution that promised an end to death,

LENIN RETURNED FROM EXILE CALLING FOR THE SOVIETS TO SEIZE POWER.

ALEXANDER KERENSKY

destruction, and hunger; the peasants would support a revolution that promised them land. And once the Russians set up a socialist state, other nations would follow their example, and socialism would spread all over the world.

Lenin hammered home his points, and the Bolsheviks accepted his policy. So did some of the Mensheviks. One of them was Leon Trotsky, who in May returned to Russia from exile in the United States. Trotsky quickly became one of the leading figures among the Bolsheviks, second only to Lenin. Putting the new policy into action, the Bolsheviks set out to gain control of the soviets and win over the people. They sent agitators to speak to the soldiers at the front and to the workers in the factories. Everywhere they brought their message: "Peace, bread, land! All power to the soviets!" And, indeed, it seemed as if this was the message the people had been waiting for. Workers took over factories, peasants took over land from the landowners, soldiers set up soviets of their own and thousands deserted from the army.

In July, great crowds, led by the Bolsheviks, poured into the streets of Petrograd in an uprising against the provisional government. But Kerensky called in troops who were still loyal to the government, and, after some fighting, the uprising was put down. Lenin was forced to flee to Finland, while Trotsky and several other Bolshevik leaders were jailed. But this set-back proved to be only temporary. The soviets were growing stronger, and it was the Bolsheviks they were supporting, not the Mensheviks or the Social Revolutionaries. Trotsky was released from prison, and became the head of a military committee. Lenin, disguising himself by shaving off his beard and putting on a wig, slipped back into Russia.

The Bolsheviks tirelessly spread their message: "Peace, bread, land! All power to the soviets!" Workers were armed. Trotsky, a fiery orator, kept winning over the soldiers, including the important garrison at St. Peter and Paul fortress in Petrograd. The soviets had set up their headquarters at the Marinsky Institute, formerly a school for girls of aristocratic families. Here, too, in what had been classrooms and assembly halls, the Bolshevik leaders met. By October, they were again planning an uprising. It was time for them to make their great bid for power.

Except for the actual date of the uprising,

ARMED WORKERS AND SOLDIERS SEIZED THE WINTER PALACE IN PETROGRAD.

there was no real secret about the Bolsheviks' plans. People came and went continually at the Marinsky Institute. Workers' and soldiers' delegations held meetings at which Lenin, Trotsky, and other Bolsheviks spoke. And yet Kerensky, who now firmly controlled the provisional government, did nothing to stop what everyone knew was coming.

The reason was that both Kerensky and the provisional government were weak. He had no strong support. As Russia's military failures continued and its armies became demoralized, the military and landowning groups opposed Kerensky more and more. The various parties in the government could not agree and quarreled among themselves. Even worse, they hesitated to take drastic action against the landowners and distribute land to the peasants. They were doing nothing to get Russia out of the war, and not enough to improve the condition of the workers. Furthermore, Kerensky was unwilling to do anything that might be thought to be opposed to freedom. But the Russians had never known real freedom and were not too interested in it now. They wanted peace, bread, and land, and were ready to follow the party that promised to give them these things. They turned to the Bolsheviks, who seemed to have a clear, direct program—and so a small group of determined men was able to win the rule of a vast country.

On November 7, those determined men were ready to give the signal for an uprising. Early in the morning, the sound of rifle shots rang out in Petrograd, and the Bolshevik revolution began. There was some serious fighting, but not much more bloodshed than there had been in the March Revolution. Many residents of the city went about their business as though nothing unusual was happening. Clerks and stenographers looked out of office windows to see men firing rifles in the street and lifeless bodies lying on the cobblestones. In the street, people were going to the theater, the movies, and the opera.

But the Smolny Institute buzzed and hummed with excitement, for the plans that had been made there were now being carried out. Armed workers arrested the ministers of the provisional government and chased the members of the Duma home. They took over important buildings, like the power plant and the Winter Palace. In Moscow, the Bolsheviks won the Kremlin, then lost it, then won it again. John Reed, an American journalist who was on the scene, called the ten days that began on November 7 "ten days that shook the world."

At times, during those ten days, it looked as though the Bolsheviks might not succeed. Other political groups were still active and trying to win the people over to their ideas. But when the ten days were over, Kerensky had fled the country, the provisional government was no more, and the Bolsheviks were in power. As the first snow of winter fell on the land, Russia entered a new age.

Peace—and Civil War
1917-1924

SPEAKING BEFORE the Congress of Soviets on November 8, the second day of the November revolution, Lenin had said, "We shall now proceed to construct the Socialist order."

But constructing any kind of order in a vast country like Russia would not be easy. The Bolsheviks had won the support of the soviets, but could they win the support of all Russia? As a matter of fact, not all the people in the country known as Russia were Russians. The tsars had gathered in under their rule many territories. On these territories lived people of many different nationalities, each speaking a different language. Could the Bolsheviks mold them all into one socialistic state? A number of political observers believed that the Bolsheviks would be unable to hold the power they had gained. The test was the elections for the Constituent Assembly, which began in late November.

Before the revolution, the Bolsheviks had demanded a Constituent Assembly. Even before they saw the results of the elections, however, they lost their enthusiasm for it. They had still less enthusiasm when the election returns were in. The Bolsheviks won only 175 out of 707 seats. The largest number of seats went to the Social Revolutionaries, who won 410. The Bolsheviks solved the problem by using soldiers to break up the Assembly when it met in January of 1918. Lenin later excused this action by say-

1152

ing that it was a time of crisis, and that any government would have done the same to hold its power. Whether or not this was true, one thing was certain—there was no longer any democratic way to end the Bolsheviks' power. On top of this, the Bolsheviks took control of the press and set up a secret police.

One of the biggest problems now facing the Bolsheviks was getting out of the war, and they sent Trotsky to negotiate a peace treaty with Germany. The Germans demanded that the Russians give up Finland, Estonia, Latvia, Lithuania, the Ukraine, and other territories. Altogether, it meant that Russia would lose one-fourth of its territory, one-third of its population, and at least half of its industries. The Russians would not agree to this. They drew out the negotiations, hoping to be saved by further revolutions in Europe. But Germany wanted a quick settlement and ordered its troops to advance into Russia. When they threatened to reach Petrograd, the Bolshevik government moved to Moscow, which became the capital of the country.

Afraid that Germany might gobble up still more of Russia, the Bolsheviks finally agreed to the terms. They signed the treaty in the city of Brest-Litovsk, on March 3, 1918. Later, after Germany had lost the war, the Treaty of Brest-Litovsk was annulled and Russia was given back much of the territory it had lost; meanwhile, it was a bitter thing for the Russians to swallow. At the same time, the Bolsheviks could point out that they had kept their promise and made peace with Germany.

REDS AGAINST WHITES

They had made peace—and yet there would still be war. For one thing, the Allies who were fighting Germany decided to intervene in Russia, and troops from Britain, the United States, France, and Japan were soon on Russian soil. There were never very many of them and they were no real danger. The real danger to the Bolsheviks came from the "White" Russian armies organized by Generals Kolchak, Denikin, and Yudenich to fight against the new government. They were supported by the people who wanted a return of the monarchy.

There had been comparatively little bloodshed during the November revolution; the civil war that now raged in Russia more than made up for it. The Bolsheviks' Red Army, led by Trotsky, fought back fiercely against the Whites. It was a cruel and terrible time, a time of horrors and atrocities committed by both sides. But the Whites could not agree among themselves. Besides, the chief concern of many of them was to win back their own lands, which had been seized by the Bolsheviks. For this reason they failed to get the support of the peasants. The peasants had no great love for the Bolsheviks, either, but without them the Whites could not hope to be successful. At first the Bolsheviks were defeated, but Trotsky proved to be a brilliant military leader, and by the middle of 1920, the Bolsheviks had won the civil war.

By this time, too, several other important things had happened. The Bolsheviks had officially adopted a new name, the Communist Party. In the summer of 1918, members of the soviet at Ekaterinberg had killed the former Tsar Nicholas and his family; five of the killers were later executed. That same summer, Social Revolutionary terrorists had tried to kill Lenin, wounding him in the neck. And in 1919, the Communist International, also known as the Comintern, was set up as an organization of Communist parties with the goal of speeding the revolutionary triumph of communism all over the world.

Stalin Succeeds Lenin
1924-1939

AFTER THE PEACE with Germany, Lenin had hoped for a breathing spell which would give him the chance to build up his backward country. Instead, there had been civil war, and it left Russia worse off than ever. Although the government had taken over all the industries, they were producing very little. A way had to be found to give the people the necessities of life, especially food. To do this, Lenin proposed to put into effect something he called the New Economic

Stalin Succeeds Lenin

Policy, soon known as NEP. While large industries would remain in the hands of the state, small businessmen could operate on their own, and peasants could sell farm products to the consumer.

To many people, including some in his own party, this seemed like a return to capitalism. Lenin denied it. He said that NEP was only a temporary measure to allow the country to get back on its feet. Besides, Marxism was not a set of rules to be followed blindly. Marxists must always adapt themselves to the circumstances of life. In spite of the opposition, Lenin succeeded in winning support for his plan, and the New Economic Policy was in effect from 1921 to 1928.

Food remained an urgent problem. Crops were poor in 1922, and there was famine in the land. Several million persons died of hunger, and the number might have been greater if aid had not arrived from the people of the United States. Even so, the New Economic Policy was working out well. Conditions were beginning to improve, and in 1923 the Communist party approved the formation of the Union of Soviet Socialist Republics. The U.S.S.R., also known as the Soviet Union, included Russia, the Ukraine, White Russia, Georgia, Armenia, and Azerbaijan.

But Lenin was in poor health, and in 1922, after his second paralytic stroke, he could no longer take part in the government. He died on January 21, 1924, and the world wondered what would happen next in Russia. Lenin had helped to change the course of history. Many people did not like that change, but on one thing most of them agreed—Lenin had not been interested in glory and power for himself. No matter how mistaken he may have been, he had done what he believed was best for Russia and the world.

THE UNION OF SOVIET SOCIALIST REPUBLICS, FORMED IN 1923

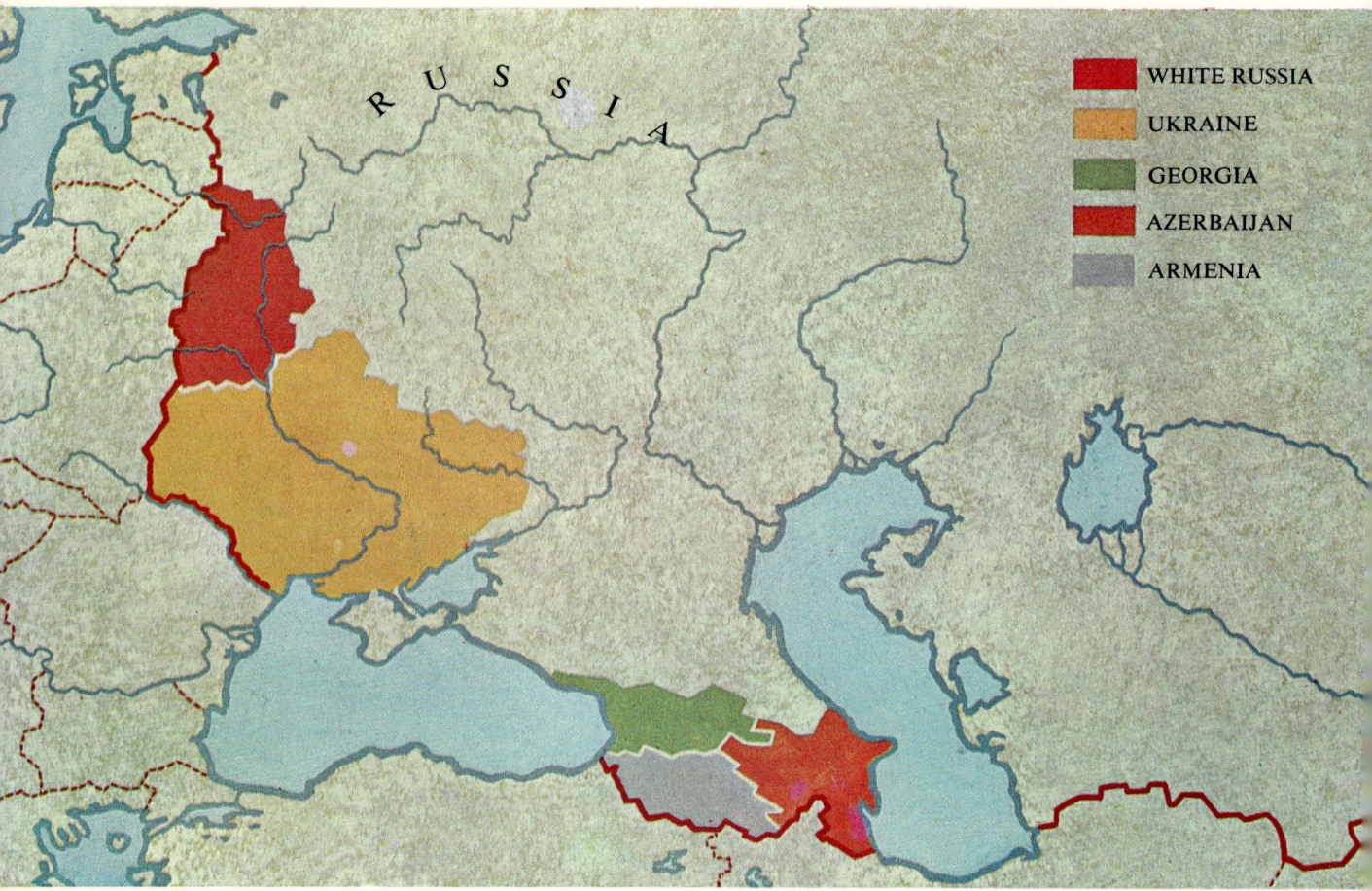

LENIN DISTRUSTED STALIN BUT WAS UNABLE TO PREVENT HIS RISE TO POWER.

Later, Winston Churchill said of Lenin, "He alone could have found the way back. . . . The Russian people were left floundering. . . . Their worst misfortune was his birth . . . their next worst—his death."

The big question now was: Who would take Lenin's place? There were no laws or rules to serve as a guide in choosing a new head of the Communist party and the Soviet Union. Next to Lenin, Trotsky had been the most important person in the party, and he seemed to be the natural choice. It must have seemed so to Trotsky himself, for he took no special steps to win the support of other party members. There was one man, however, who did not hesitate to play politics and line up supporters for himself. He was the General Secretary of the party, and his name was Joseph Stalin.

Joseph Stalin was not, strictly speaking, a Russian. He was a native of Georgia, a land on the Black Sea that had been taken over by the tsars several centuries before. Born in 1879, he was the son of a shoemaker named Dzhugashvili. He studied to be a priest, but while still a student he became interested in Marxism. He was expelled from the religious seminary, and, at the age of seventeen, began working for the Social Democrats. Soon he took the name Stalin, which means "made of steel." Unlike many other revolutionists, he spent little time in exile in foreign lands. A devoted follower of Lenin since 1903, he was arrested five times, and each time he managed to escape. Then, in 1913, the tsarist government exiled him for life to Siberia, but he was released after the revolution in March of 1917. With most of the Bolshevik leaders in exile, he became one of Lenin's most trusted representatives in Russia.

Lenin had left behind a letter in which he had written: "Comrade Stalin, having become General Secretary, has concentrated in his own hands unbounded power, and I am not sure whether he will always know how to use this power cautiously enough. . . . Stalin is too rough, and this fault, quite tolerable among ourselves and in dealings between us Communists, becomes intolerable in the office of General Secretary. Therefore I suggest that the comrades think of some means of displacing Stalin from this position and of naming in his stead some other man who will

Stalin Succeeds Lenin

THIS PAINTING SHOWS STALIN SPEAKING TO FACTORY WORKERS IN 1924.

differ from Comrade Stalin only in this dominant characteristic, i.e., will be more tolerant, more loyal, more civil and more considerate toward comrades, less capricious, etc."

When Lenin died, Stalin was almost unknown outside his own country. Russian communists considered him a good organizer, but not much of a thinker. By skillful political maneuvering, and by using his power as general secretary of the party, Stalin made himself the real head of the party. And, because the party controlled the government, he also became the head of the Soviet Union. That was in 1924, and before long he would show that he was indeed "made of steel."

A disagreement began to develop between Stalin and Trotsky. The Bolsheviks had expected that, after Russia's revolution, there would be similar revolutions in other parts of the world, particularly in Europe. While there had been a great deal of unrest, revolutions had taken place only in Germany and Hungary, and these had been put down. The Soviet Union, as vast as it was, remained the only communist state in the world. Could communism possibly succeed in one nation that was surrounded on all sides by capitalist nations? Trotsky said that it was impossible. Unless there were revolutions elsewhere, the Soviet Union could not survive. Stalin, on the other hand, said that this was nonsense. Communism could be built in one nation, and the Soviet Union would not fail. By this time, Stalin had made himself dictator, and his view became the official view of the Communist party and of the government. Trotsky refused to change his mind, and in 1927 he and some of his followers were expelled from the party. Early

Stalin Succeeds Lenin

in 1929, Stalin forced Trotsky to leave the Soviet Union and go into exile.

Meanwhile, Stalin was going ahead with his program of building communism in one country. In 1928 he announced a Five-Year Plan to increase industrial production. Russia was a backward country, but Stalin proposed to bring its industry up to the level of the capitalist countries in one generation. Russia must first build up its heavy industry—power plants, steel mills, factories that produced machinery, and means of transportation. Only after that had been accomplished could Russia build up the industries producing consumer goods, such as shoes, clothing, and furniture. The people must do without comforts. They must make sacrifices in the present for the sake of the future, for the sake of their children's future.

At the same time, Stalin put an end to the New Economic Policy and set up a new policy for the peasants. They could no longer work their own small plots of ground. Instead, their farms would be combined into large "collective" farms, run by the government almost like factories. Under the New Economic Policy, a number of peasants had become *kulaks*—well-to-do farmers who owned their own land, implements, and farm animals. Stalin intended to do away with the *kulaks* and took strong measures against them. The *kulaks* fought back in every way they could, but Stalin was determined to wipe them out. Millions were executed, imprisoned, or taken from their homes and sent to other parts of the country.

As the first Five-Year Plan drew to a close, the government announced that it was a success and immediately began another. Stalin continued to have trouble with the peasants and with farm production, but otherwise his policies seemed to be working. Politically, he was in a stronger position than ever. He had defeated Trotsky and was gaining more power every year.

And yet Stalin was not satisfied. In 1934, the world was shocked by the first of the "purge" trials. A number of old Bolsheviks were accused of plotting to overthrow the government and of having been spies or traitors. They were put on trial, and, strangely enough, they all publicly confessed to their crimes. The world could not help wondering why, for these were men who had sacrificed much for the revolution and had worked side by side with Lenin. Many explanations were offered—they had been tortured, their spirit had been broken by imprisonment, their families had been threatened. Whatever the reason for their confessions, they were found guilty and executed. The first purge trials were followed by others, and when they were over there were few old Bolsheviks left in the government. Thousands of other less important persons were also executed or sent to prison or labor camps.

There was now no one to seriously challenge

LEON TROTSKY

Stalin Succeeds Lenin

Stalin's position. He was the dictator of the Soviet Union and the unquestioned leader of the international communist movement. Although he seldom appeared in public, pictures and statues of him were everywhere, almost like the old icons. History books were rewritten to show that he was a hero and that Trotsky and other old Bolsheviks had done little for the revolution, or had even been its enemy. The government revolved around Stalin. He liked to work late at night, and so other officials also worked at night, and the lights in the Kremlin burned until the early hours of morning.

Outside the Soviet Union, there were differences of opinion among students of politics about Marx's teachings, but most agreed that he had dreamed of a better world—a world of freedom and plenty for all people. Men had fought and died—and many were still willing to fight and die—for that dream. Stalin, too, said he believed in that dream and insisted that he was following the teachings of Marx. But in the Soviet Union, under Stalin, the dream was turning into a nightmare. Marx had called for a dictatorship of the working class; the Soviet Union had a dictatorship of the Communist party, and Stalin ruled the party. Marx had said that the government would in time wither away; in the Soviet Union, the government was growing stronger, and Stalin ruled the government. Marx had spoken of freedom and liberty; in the Soviet Union, Stalin's secret police spread terror and tens of thousands of people were killed or imprisoned.

Stalin gave the Soviet Union a constitution that promised democracy, but only one political party was allowed and at elections there was only a single slate of candidates. Stalin opened up opportunities for education, but he kept strict control of the schools, as well as of science and the arts. Russia no longer had a tsar. It had no aristocracy, no rich landowners, no millionaires, and yet in many ways the Russia of Stalin resembled the Russia of the tsars.

At the same time, Stalin was accomplishing what he had set out to do. He was building up industry, building up the army, building up the nation. The cost in human lives and misery and suffering was enormous, but he was molding the Soviet Union into one of the world's great powers.

AS DICTATOR OF THE SOVIET UNION, STALIN FORCED THOUSANDS OF "KULAKS"—THE MORE PROSPEROUS PEASANTS—OFF THEIR LAND.

1158

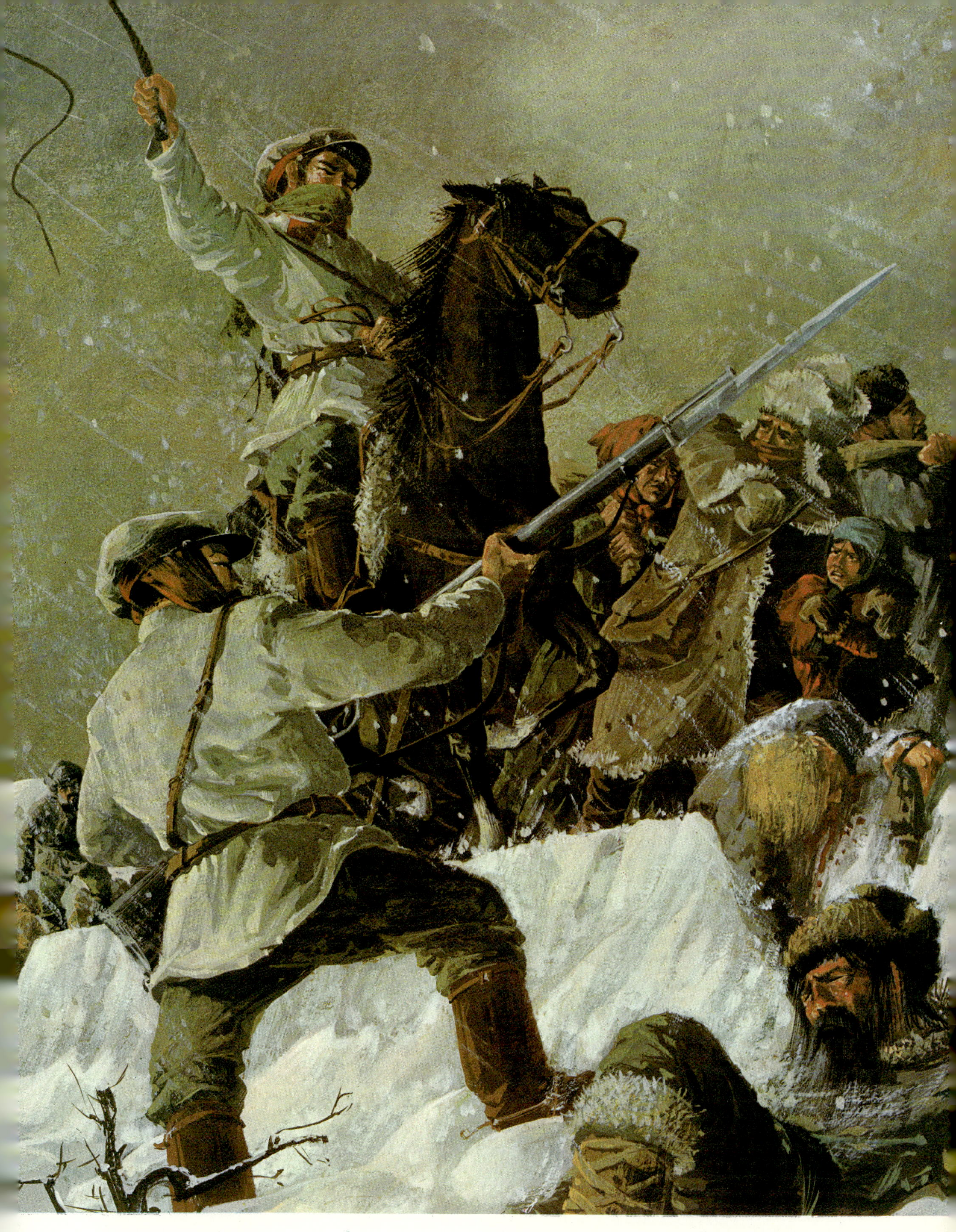

Fascism and Mussolini

1918-1936

WHILE THE red flag with its emblem of communism—the hammer and sickle—flew over the domes of the Kremlin in Moscow, other new flags were being unfurled in Europe. The end of World War I left the leaders of Italy dissatisfied. They had hoped—and expected—to get rich territories as a reward for joining the war on the side of the Allies and fighting against Germany. But when the statesmen of the Allies divided the spoils of war, Italy got practically nothing.

The Italian soldiers, returning from the front, found their homecoming anything but sweet. Prices were rising every day. Jobs were scarce and growing scarcer. The government was deeply in debt. Neither the king, little Victor Emmanuel III, nor the parliament, the Chamber of Deputies, seemed able to do anything to better conditions. The Socialists pointed out that they had predicted exactly what was happening—and the people listened. Following the example of the Russian Marxists, the Socialists called for action—and the people acted. A great wave of strikes swept the country. Farmers tried to seize land. Crowds of workers tramped through the streets singing "Bandiera Rossa," a song of the red flag waving triumphantly for socialism and liberty.

Communists and anarchists were also busy preaching revolution, and for a while it looked as though Italy would go the same way as Russia. In 1920, during August and September, workers took over more than 600 factories. Italians wondered: Was this the revolution? Would Italy soon have a communist dictatorship? But when the government agreed to set up factory councils, the workers listened to the more moderate Socialists and gave up the factories.

Even so, the aristocrats and landowners and industrialists were worried. They had escaped revolution this time, but it had come close—too close. Next time the red flag might indeed fly triumphantly over all of Italy. What the country

TENS OF THOUSANDS WERE ASSEMBLED FOR MUSSOLINI'S MASS MEETINGS IN ROME.

ment that would gain Italy a place among the great powers of the world. Then, in 1920, after the workers had given up the factories they had seized, he showed what he really wanted. In his newspaper, he attacked the communists with fiery words. In the streets, his Black Shirts—bands of young men who wore black shirts as a sort of uniform—attacked the communists with clubs and other weapons. They invented a new kind of torture, forcing their victims to swallow huge doses of castor oil. They wrecked the headquarters of trade unions and destroyed the printing presses of newspapers that opposed Mussolini. The government did nothing to stop them; in fact, it quietly helped them.

The big landowners and wealthy industrialists welcomed Mussolini and approved of his Black Shirts. Here, at last, was someone who knew how to take action against communists and rebellious workers. Others, too, supported Mussolini—people who were tired of a weak government, people who were tired of the quarrels among the various political parties, people who were tired of confusion and uncertainty.

needed was a leader, a strong man who would stop the Communists, put the workers in their place, and make Italy a powerful and respected nation. To their relief and joy, they found such a man. He was a former socialist named Benito Mussolini.

Mussolini was born in 1883; his father was a village blacksmith, his mother a schoolteacher. Mussolini, too, became a schoolteacher, then went to Switzerland for further study. Expelled from Switzerland for socialist activity, he returned to Italy and to teaching. But it was politics that interested him. By the time World War I broke out, he had become a professional revolutionist, had served a short prison term, and was editor of the Italian Socialist party's newspaper. Like most Italian socialists, Mussolini was opposed to the war. Suddenly, however, he changed his mind, and to spread his views he set up his own newspaper. He was called up to the army and served as a private until 1917, when he was wounded. After his discharge, he went back to his paper.

Mussolini soon had a number of followers, to whom he preached something that sounded like socialism. But he also called for a strong govern-

MUSSOLINI LOVED FANCY UNIFORMS.

Fascism and Mussolini

In 1921, Mussolini organized his followers into the Fascist party. It took its name from the party's emblem, the *fasces*—a bundle of rods containing an axe. The *fasces* had been an emblem of power in ancient Rome, and Mussolini promised that he would bring back to Italy the glory that once was Rome's. Members of the Fascist party greeted each other with the old "Roman salute," right hand and arm upraised, and Mussolini was called *Il Duce,* the leader.

As the Fascist party grew, Mussolini demanded more and more power in the government. In October of 1922, he told a huge meeting of fascists in Naples that "either the government will be given to us or we shall seize it by marching on Rome." Later that same month, Mussolini ordered his Black Shirts to advance on Rome. The "march" turned out to be something of a joke. Although Mussolini would later refer to it as a splendid and heroic victory, there was little opposition to the fascists. The king allowed them to enter the city, and he appointed Mussolini premier, as he had the legal right to do. The way was wide open for Mussolini to become dictator of Italy.

Within a few years, Mussolini took the title of "Head of the Government." In 1928, the constitution was rewritten and fascism became the official political system of Italy. Mussolini controlled the parliament and all the military

A CROWD CHEERS MUSSOLINI AND MEMBERS OF HIS STAFF IN 1922.

forces. He controlled the schools, the universities, the press, the labor unions. There was only one political party—the Fascist party. There was no freedom of speech or of assembly. To round up those opposed to fascism, there was a secret police. For punishment, there were imprisonment, beatings, castor oil, and sometimes death.

Industries were also regulated. They were divided into twenty-two groups, called corporations, covering such fields as mining, oil, chemicals, and clothing. The arts and professions, the theater and the tourist trade were covered as well. The corporations were under the control of a committee and a minister, who in turn were under the control of Mussolini. This system was know as the "corporate state." In spite of certain restrictions, the millionaires remained millionaires. The landowners still owned their land, the industrialists still owned their mills and mines and factories, and both landowners and industrialists still collected their profits. At the same time, the government fixed the wages of workers and outlawed strikes. Not for nothing had the rich welcomed Mussolini and given the fascists their support. True, Italy no longer had any civil liberties, but neither did it have communism, and the workers had been put in their place.

And so Mussolini had given the world a new word—fascism—and a new kind of political movement. Fascism proclaimed that the state was everything, the individual nothing. As Mussolini put it, "Everything in the state, nothing outside the state, nothing against the state." For the people who lived under fascist rule, he made a simple motto: "Work, fight, obey."

A CONQUERING CAESAR

By threatening and blustering, Mussolini won some diplomatic successes. He recovered some small territories that Italy had once occupied and then lost. Inside Italy, conditions were at first a little better. Foreign visitors sympathetic to fascism said that Mussolini had brought order to Italy. He had at least made the trains run on time, and he was teaching the easy-going Italians modern efficiency. And the mass meetings of the fascists were exciting. His large jaw jutting out, his dark eyes glaring, Mussolini spoke to his followers from the balcony of the Palazzo Venezia in Rome. Their hands raised in salute, they chanted, "Du-ce! Du-ce! Du-ce!"

HAILE SELASSIE'S PALACE GUARDS

But if Mussolini was to bring back the glorious days of the Roman Empire, he had to be another Caesar—and to be Caesar, he had to make war. So, in 1935, he attacked the little Negro kingdom of Ethiopia in Africa. Its ruler, dignified, bearded Haile Selassie, appealed for help to the League of Nations. The League did try to stop Mussolini, but the action it took was not very effective, and Mussolini went on with his war. There was never a doubt about how it would end. With cannon, tanks, planes, bombs, and poison gas, he attacked the Ethiopian capital. The Ethiopians had no cannon, no tanks, no planes, no bombs, no poison gas, and few weapons of any kind.

In May of 1936, his jaw jutting even more fiercely, his eyes bulging with pride, Mussolini boasted of his great victory. "Ethiopia is Italian!" he told a huge crowd. "Du-ce! Du-ce! Du-ce!" the crowd chanted, while Mussolini stood on the balcony like a conquering Caesar.

But there were other men in Europe who would carry the violence and terror of fascism even further.

THE LEADERS OF THE 1923 BEER HALL PUTSCH. TO THE LEFT OF HITLER IS LUDENDORFF.

Revolution in a Beer Hall

1923-1924

ON NOVEMBER 8, 1923, about three thousand men were sitting at the tables of a large beer hall on the outskirts of Munich. They had come this evening not just to drink beer; they were to hear a speech by Gustave von Kahr. He was the head of the government of Bavaria, one of the states of Germany. Conditions had been bad in Germany since the end of World War I, and Kahr's audience was anxious to learn what the government intended to do.

Kahr was still speaking when there was a commotion at the back of the hall. Several men had come in, and one of them leaped up on a table and fired a pistol into the air. He wore his hair combed down over one eye and had a small moustache that resembled Charlie Chaplin's. Kahr recognized him. His name was Adolph Hitler. He was the head of a political group, the National Socialist German Workers party, whose members were usually called Nazis.

Hitler and his companions pushed their way to the speaker's platform, where Hitler shouted, "The National Revolution has begun!" The building was surrounded by his brown-shirted storm troopers, their machine guns ready. Soon, he said, the Nazi flag with its black swastika would be flying over Bavaria. Then the Nazis would march on Berlin and take over all of Germany.

As it happened, Hitler was a bit too optimistic. He would not take over Germany quite that soon. Forcing Kahr and two other important government officials into a back room, Hitler threatened them with his pistol. He thought he had won them over and could expect their help, but again he was mistaken. In the confusion they managed to slip away, and Kahr issued an order dissolving the Nazi party.

The next day, disappointed but still hopeful, Hitler led 3,000 of his storm troopers against the building of the War Ministry. It was guarded by a detachment of armed police, who refused

IN 1923, WHEN ARMED POLICE FIRED ON NAZI STORM TROOPERS TRYING TO TAKE THE WAR MINISTRY BUILDING IN MUNICH, HITLER FLED TO A CAR THAT CARRIED HIM TO SAFETY, BUT HE WAS LATER JAILED.

to give way. A shot was fired—by which side, no one knew—and firing by both sides followed. Although the shooting lasted for no more than a minute, sixteen Nazis and three policemen were killed, and a number wounded. Like the other Nazis, Hitler had immediately thrown himself to the ground to avoid being hit, and he was the first to get up and run to safety. Reaching a car that was waiting for him, he was driven off to the house of a friend.

During the next few days, the police searched for the Nazi leaders. Two of them, Herman Goering and Rudolph Hess, escaped to Austria. Hitler and the rest were arrested and jailed. The beer hall revolution, which became known as the "beer hall *putsch*," had failed. But Germany—and the world—had not heard the last of Adolph Hitler.

AT LEFT, HITLER AS A CORPORAL

CORPORAL HITLER

In February of 1924, Hitler went on trial for high treason. Newspapermen from various countries were in the courtroom, and Hitler saw that this was his chance to make himself known far beyond Bavaria. The judges had received their instructions from the Minister of Justice, who was a friend and supporter of Hitler, and they let him do much as he pleased. Often he spoke for hours at a time. He attacked the government of Germany, predicted that it would be overthrown, and proclaimed that the country would be ruled by the Nazis. The judges found him guilty, and by law the punishment for high treason was life imprisonment. But he was given a sentence of five years, and he would actually be freed in less than nine months.

The trial was widely reported and it made Hitler's name known throughout the world. People began to wonder: Who was this strange man with the little moustache and his hair combed down over one eye? What did he want? Where did he come from?

Although he had said that someday he would be ruler of all Germany, Hitler was not a German. He was a citizen of Austria, where he had been born, near the German border, on April 20, 1889. His father was a customs official of little importance. Hitler failed to graduate from high school, but his best subject was drawing, and his ambition was to be a painter. Twice he applied for admission to the Vienna Academy of Fine Arts, and twice he was turned down. He was told that he simply did not have enough talent to become an artist.

At the age of twenty, after both his father and his mother had died, Hitler settled in Vienna. For the next four years he lived the life of a vagabond and was often hungry. He did all sorts of odd jobs. Among other things, he painted and sold crude pictures of Viennese scenes and commercial posters. Shabby and dirty, he was already beginning to form the ideas which would later influence so many people. He considered himself a German, and he had a strong feeling for Germany as a nation. Just as strong were his feelings about Marxists and Jews. He hated them both, especially the Jews.

Leaving Vienna, Hitler went to Germany, where he was living when World War I began in 1914. He welcomed the war and volunteered for the army. Here was his chance to serve the country he admired so much. Besides, in the army he would no longer be an outcast. Later he wrote, "I sank down on my knees and thanked Heaven out of the fullness of my heart for granting me the good fortune of being permitted to live in such a time. . . ."

Hitler proved to be a good soldier. Although he never rose above the rank of corporal, he was given a medal—the Iron Cross, First Class—for bravery. He was once wounded in the leg, and shortly before the end of the war he was temporarily blinded by gas. He was still in the hospital when he learned that Germany had surrendered and the kaiser had given up his throne.

How was it possible? How could it have happened? How had the great and mighty Germany gone down to defeat? Shocked and horrified, Hitler burst into tears.

"My Struggle"

When Hitler was discharged by the army in 1918, he found an altogether different Germany from the one he had known before the war. It was no longer ruled by a kaiser. The Socialists had taken over the government, but the Communists were active and calling for a revolution like that of Russia's. After some fighting, the government succeeded in putting down the Communists. Their leaders, Karl Liebknecht and Rosa Luxemburg, were killed, and the communist threat died down, at least for a time.

In 1919, after elections, a coalition—a combination of various parties—led by the Socialists, took control of the government. It set up a republic, which was called the "Weimar Republic," because the government first met in the city of Weimar. A constitution was adopted, and it looked as though Germany was on the way to becoming a real democracy.

But there were too many people in Germany who had no use for democracy. Germany had long been a militaristic nation, and the army had had enormous power. Its officers longed to regain that power, and they were supported by the judges and officials whom the republic inherited from the old government. The army began to spread the story that it was not to blame for losing the war. Germany should have won, and would have won—if it had not been for the Socialists and the other politicians who wanted to set up a republic. They had plotted against the army, they had "stabbed it in the back." They were responsible for Germany's defeat, for the signing of the harsh Versailles Treaty, for all of Germany's troubles.

The story was not true, but millions of Germans were ready to believe it. Like Hitler, they had been shocked by their country's surrender, and they were looking for someone to blame. Besides, it was getting harder and harder for them just to eat and stay alive. The government was in deep financial trouble; the value of its money kept falling. Before the war, 4.2 German marks had been worth one American dollar. After the war, it dropped to 7,000 to the dollar, then to 50,000, to 160,000, to 1,100,000. By the end of 1923, the mark was between 2,520,000,000,000 and 4,000,000,000,000 to the dollar, and thousands of people were ruined. The big industrialists, however, paid off debts with this cheap money, built up their plants, and made huge profits. But they were afraid of communism and did not trust the republic. They, too, were among the enemies of democracy.

This was the kind of Germany to which Hitler returned—a Germany of poverty, unrest, political plotting, and even political murder. Unknown and with little money, Hitler arrived in Munich. He joined a small, unimportant political party, and was soon convinced that he had at last found an occupation that really suited him. He learned that he had great ability at public speaking. He could rouse people, excite them, stir them up. He was just as skillful at playing politics. The little party he joined became the Nazi party, and Hitler was its head. He organized his *Sturmabteilung,* the brown-shirted storm troopers, who guarded his meetings and broke up the meetings of other parties. He adopted the swastika as the Nazi emblem. He was joined by some of the men who would be closely associated with him in the years to come—Rudolf Hess, Herman Goering, Ernst Roehm. His beer hall revolution was a failure, but he turned his trial for high treason into a triumph, even though he was found guilty.

Nor did he waste the time he spent in prison. He served his sentence in the fortress at Landsberg, where he was treated more as a guest than as a prisoner. He was given a room of his own, and there he dictated a book—*My Struggle,* or, in German, *Mein Kampf.* In it he gave his ideas and outlined his plans, and it became the bible of the Nazis.

THE MASTER RACE

Hitler was not a good writer, and he wandered from one subject to another, but certain of his ideas stood out. One was that the Germans were "the highest species of humanity" on earth, and must be the master race of the world.

A GERMAN PAINTING OF HITLER AS A KNIGHT IN ARMOR

Hitler said the Germans belonged to what he called the "Aryan" race, and that they must "care for the purity of the blood." In other words, they must not marry "non-Aryans," the members of other races. If the Germans were to be masters, they must have servants. They would be served particularly by the Slavic peoples—the Russians, the Czechs, and the Poles. Some races, particularly the Jews, were not even fit to serve the Germans, and must be wiped out.

And how would the master race remain master? By force, by conquest, by war. "Mankind has grown great in eternal struggle," said Hitler, "and only in eternal peace does it perish." War was a good thing, and only through war could nations achieve greatness. Furthermore, the master race must expand beyond Germany and it needed more space for living—in German, *Lebensraum*. Germany would first take over the countries with large German populations, such as Austria and parts of Poland and Czechoslovakia. Then it would take over the vast lands of Russia. This would also do away with the Bolsheviks and be a blow to the Jews. According to Hitler, the Bolsheviks and the international communist movement were under the control of the Jews.

When the Nazis had set up their own *Reich*, or state, there would be no such "nonsense" as democracy. At the head of the government, at the head of the nation and the people, would be a *Fuehrer*, or leader—an absolute dictator. This, of course, would be Hitler himself. Below him would be less important leaders, who would take orders from above and pass them on to those below. The people would obey, because their worship of the *Fuehrer* would be a kind of religion. And, for those who would not obey, there would be terror and torture and death.

Here, in *Mein Kampf*, a book that anyone could pick up and read, was Hitler's plan to conquer Germany—and the world.

Fire in the Reichstag
1923-1933

DURING THE years that followed Hitler's adventure in the Munich beer hall, ministers came and went in the German government. Among them were some able men, particularly Gustave Stresemann. He was foreign minister from 1923 until his death in 1929. His policy was to work out a way of getting along with Germany's former enemies, so that Germany's mighty industrial machine could operate again as it had in the past.

This policy brought results. Inflation was stopped, and foreign bankers made large loans to German industry. Smoke poured from the smokestacks of Germany's efficiently run factories, and the republic began to prosper. It looked as though history had taken a new turn—a turn that would leave Hitler forgotten.

And then came 1929. A great depression had begun in Europe and the United States, and Germany's recovery was at an end. There were no more foreign loans for German industry, and few markets for its goods. The wheels of factories stopped turning, thousands of people were thrown out of work, and long breadlines stretched

HITLER TAKES A NAZI SALUTE FROM STORM TROOPS AND BLACK-CLAD ELITE GUARDS.

Fire in the Reichstag

through the streets of the cities. The Germans had just begun to forget the terrible days of inflation, and now they faced days that might be just as terrible, or even worse. The government seemed helpless, and so they turned to the communists—and to Adolph Hitler and the Nazis.

And Hitler was ready. He had his brown-shirted storm troopers, and his black-shirted SS men—the *Schutzstaffel,* his specially picked and trusted soldiers and guards. To help carry out his orders, he had fat Herman Goering, serious Ernst Roehm, and meek-looking Heinrich Himmler. He also had Dr. Joseph Goebbels, a small, dark, well-educated man with a limp, who would prove to be a master of propaganda. For the people, Hitler had promises, all kinds of promises. He would give jobs to the jobless. He would bring back prosperity. He would refuse to abide by the terms of the Versailles Treaty. He would control the bankers and industrialists. He would build Germany into the greatest nation in the world. With his promises, he gave the Germans someone to blame for their troubles, someone to hate and despise—the Jews and the Marxists.

As the depression continued and the number of unemployed mounted to more than six million, Hitler began to get money. The men who ran Germany's great steel, chemical, and coal companies, its banks and insurance companies, were afraid that the communists would take over the government. Hitler had promises for them, too, even though he had attacked them in his speeches. He would protect them from the communists; he would save them from a red revolution; he was the communists' most bitter enemy. Industrialists, bankers, and businessmen were impressed, and they gave him millions of marks to support the activities of the Nazis.

With the money, Hitler was able to reach even more of the German people. And the people listened. It made no difference to them that most of what Hitler said was lies. It made no difference to them that the Jews and the Marxists were not to blame for Germany's troubles. It made no difference to them that Hitler promised something that sounded like socialism, and meanwhile took money from bankers and industrialists. The people were hungry and fearful. They wanted a way out of the depression, and Hitler seemed to know the way. And so they listened, attending meetings that were becoming larger and larger. They raised their hands in the salute that Hitler had borrowed from Mussolini, and shouted, *"Heil Hitler!"*—"Hail Hitler!"

There were weaknesses in the government, too, that made things easier for Hitler. It clamped down hard on the communists, but it allowed Hitler's stormtroopers to do much as they pleased. There were also weaknesses in Hitler's opposition. Both the Social Democrat party and the Communist party were opposed to him. If they had united their forces, they might have been able to win more votes in the elections than the Nazis. But they did not trust each other, and they fought each other almost as much as they fought the Nazis.

Moreover, the Germans had no tradition of democracy. They had been taught to respect authority and obey orders without question. And so they listened, and believed, and shouted, *"Heil Hitler! Heil Hitler! Sieg Heil!"*

And they voted for Hitler. In almost every election held during the 1930's, the Nazis made gains over the previous election. In 1932, Hitler ran for president against General Paul von Hindenburg, a German hero of World War I. Although the chancellor was the real power in the German government, he was appointed by the president, so that post, too, was important. Hitler lost the election. He now had about 400,000 stormtroopers, and for a while he considered overthrowing the government by force. Then he decided against it. His brownshirts had to be content with street fights against Communists and Social Democrats during the election campaigns for the Reichstag, the German parliament.

By 1932, the Nazis had won 230 seats in the Reichstag—the most any party had won since the beginning of the republic. Hitler demanded that he be made chancellor. The eighty-five-year-old President Hindenburg refused, instead appointing Franz von Papen. When von Papen saw that he could not get the support of a majority of Reichstag members, he called for a new election. This time the Nazis lost 2,000,000 votes and won only 37 per cent of the total vote, while the Communists gained. Even so, the Nazis had the largest number of seats in the Reichstag, and again Hitler demanded that he be named chan-

THE REICHSTAG WAS QUICK TO GRANT HITLER THE POWERS OF A DICTATOR.

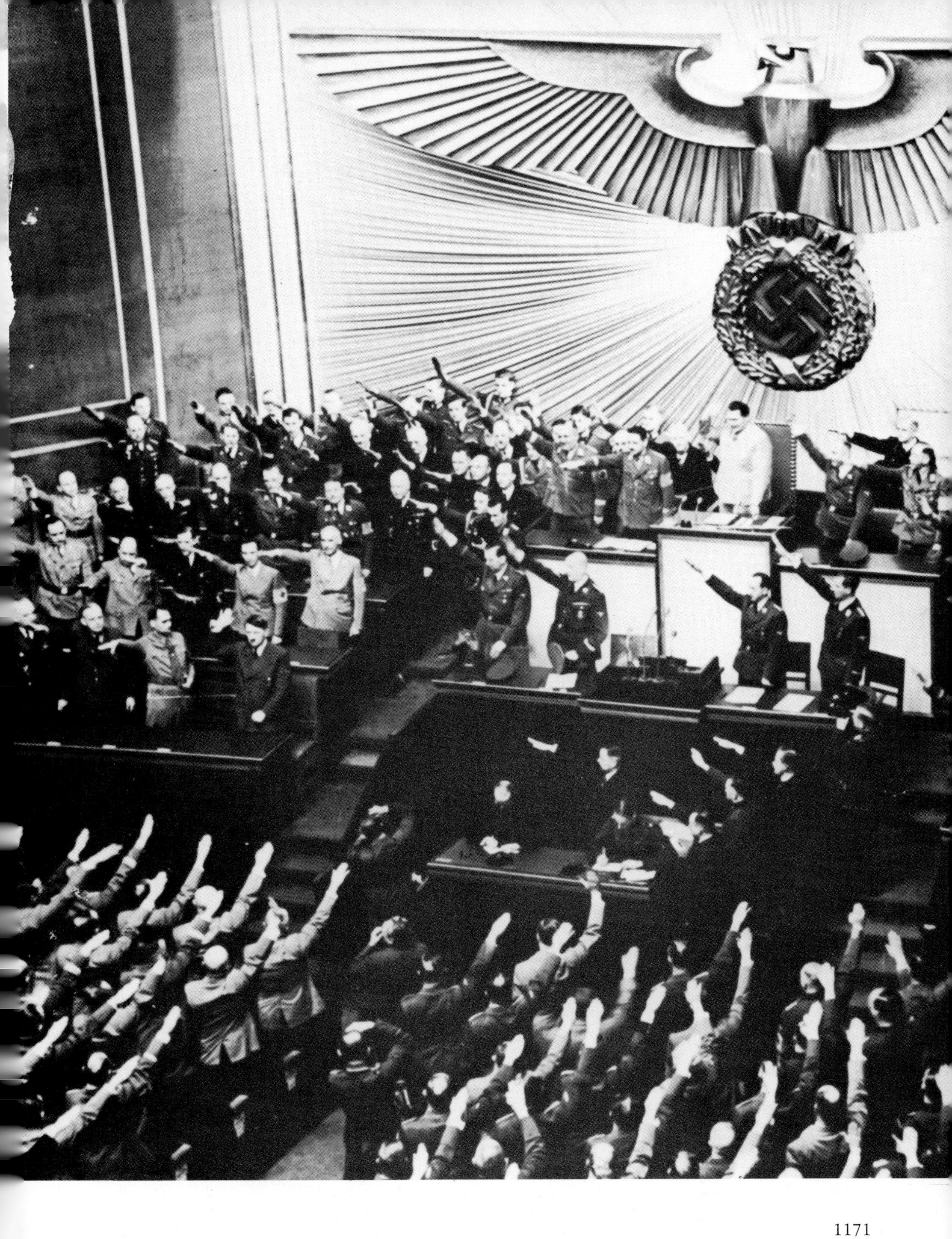

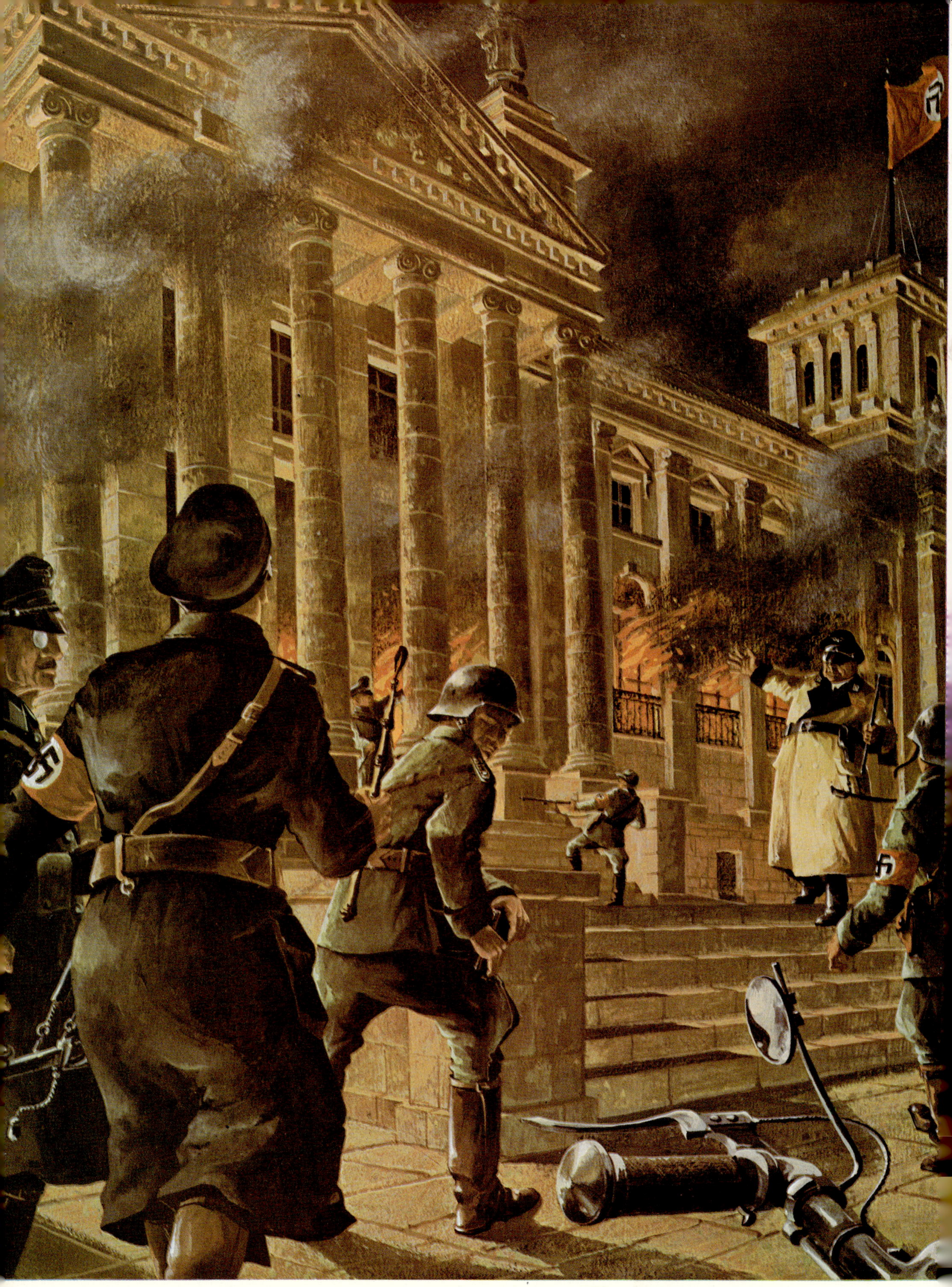

Fire in the Reichstag

cellor. Again he was turned down, because he also demanded the powers of a dictator. General Kurt von Schleicher got the post, but he, too, could not win the support of the divided parties in the Reichstag. He resigned, and at last Hindenburg appointed Hitler chancellor.

Like Mussolini in Italy, Hitler had come to power by peaceful and legal means. But he still did not have all the power he wanted. He dissolved the Reichstag, as he had the right to do as chancellor, and called for a new election to be held on March 5, 1933. The Nazis had no doubts of their success. Everything was in their favor. The leading party in the Reichstag, they now controlled the press and the government-owned radio system. Their brown-shirted hoodlums beat up Communists, Socialists, and members of Catholic trade unions. Hitler cracked down on the Communists, forbidding their meetings and closing their press. He hoped for a Communist uprising, so that he could smash it and win the full support of the people. When the Communists refused to oblige, the Nazis decided to arrange an incident and blame it on the Communists.

And so, on February 27, a cry went up in Berlin: "The Reichstag is on fire!" This was the building where the German parliament met, and an eyewitness later said its dome looked "as though it were illuminated by searchlights. Every now and again a burst of flame and a swirl of smoke blurred the outline."

A group of Nazis, led by Goering, rushed to the burning building. "This is a Communist crime against the new government!" Goering shouted. "This is the beginning of the Communist revolution! We must not wait a minute. We will show no mercy. Every Communist official must be shot where he is found. Every Communist deputy must this very night be strung up."

Goering himself had helped to plan the fire. It had been set by the Nazis, aided by a feeble-minded Dutch Communist named Marinus van der Lubbe. This half-wit was later put on trial, together with several Communist leaders, including Georgi Dimitroff, a Bulgarian. Dimitroff, who acted as his own lawyer, had no way of proving that the Nazis had set the fire. But he questioned Goering so sharply that finally the fat Nazi shrieked, "Out with you, you scoundrel!" As Dimitroff was led away, he turned and asked Goering, "Are you afraid of my questions?" Goering's reply was: "You wait until we get you outside this court, you scoundrel!"

Van der Lubbe was found guilty and beheaded; Dimitroff and the other Communists were acquitted. But that was later, after the election, and meanwhile Hitler was taking advantage of the situation. The day after the fire, he persuaded President Hindenburg to issue an emergency decree that did away with all civil liberties. The government could even open personal mail and listen in on private telephone conversations.

Hitler sent his stormtroopers to round up, torture, and beat thousands of Communists, Social Democrats, and other opponents. With the millions of marks that had been donated by the nation's biggest businesses, the Nazis were able to stage huge meetings and parades. Stormtroopers marched through the streets to the stirring music of brass bands. Crowds roared, *"Heil Hitler! Sieg Heil!"* The swastika flag flew everywhere. Hitler, Goering, and Gobbels thundered and snarled on the government-owned radio, warning against the Communist menace, attacking liberals and Jews. They played upon the people's fears, promising them a strong, proud, prosperous Germany, a Nazi heaven on earth.

With all this, the Nazis got only 44 per cent of the vote, less than a two-thirds majority. But it was enough. They won 288 seats in the Reichstag. Together with the 52 seats of the Nationalists, who also supported Hitler, they had control of the government.

On the first day the new Reichstag met, Hitler stood before its members in a Nazi uniform. Again like Mussolini, he demanded that he be given the power of a dictator for four years. The Reichstag quickly did as he asked. It was all perfectly legal, done by vote of the elected representatives of the German people. But there would be no more free elections as long as the Nazis ruled. Liberty, freedom, and decency had been destroyed as surely as the papers that had gone up in flames in the Reichstag fire. The way was open for the establishment of Germany's Third Reich, or state. The way was open for death, destruction, and terror under the banner of the swastika.

THE NAZIS BLAMED THE BURNING OF THE REICHSTAG ON THE COMMUNISTS.

Germany Under the Nazis
1933-1939

It was almost midnight in Berlin—a strange hour for a parade in any city. But down the street called *Unter den Linden* paraded thousands of students, carrying torches that flickered in the darkness. In the big square near the University of Berlin, they gathered around a great pile of books. They cheered as the books were set on fire and flames rose toward the sky. For this was the night of May 10, 1933—less than five months since Hitler had become head of the government —the night when books were being burned in a number of German cities. These were "subversive" books, "un-German" books—or so the Nazis said. They were written by more than 160 writers, including Albert Einstein, Thomas Mann, Jack London, Helen Keller, and H. G. Wells.

In the light of the bonfire, Dr. Goebbels, who was now Hitler's propaganda minister, spoke to the students. "The soul of the German people can again express itself," he said. "These flames not only illuminate the final end of an old era; they also light up the new."

There was no doubt that the "old era" had ended and that the "New Order," as Hitler called it, had come to Germany. As month followed month, Hitler gained more and more control of Germany and its people. He outlawed all political parties but his own. The state, he once said, is the Nazi party. He wiped out the trade unions. He made life more difficult for the Jews. Hitler would decide how Germans lived and worked and worshiped, and even thought. He took Germany out of the League of Nations. He made it clear that he would not abide by the Treaty of Versailles and would re-arm. Germany would again become a great military power.

And yet, some Nazis were still not satisfied. Among them was Ernst Roehm, the leader of the storm troopers. There were now two and a half million of them, and Roehm wanted them to become the basis of a new regular army. Besides, Roehm had taken seriously Hitler's socialistic talk. He called for a "second revolution" that would give Hitler's loyal followers, especially the storm troopers, a chance to get their hands on the wealth of the big industrialists and landowners. As for the storm troopers themselves, they had committed all sorts of crimes for Hitler, and now they wanted their reward.

Hitler had no intention of replacing the regular army and the aristocrats who led it. After all, the storm troopers were not trained, disciplined soldiers. They were gangs of hoodlums whose specialty was street fighting. They did well enough at bashing in the heads of Jews or breaking the bones of Communists and Socialists, but that was all. Nor did Hitler have any intention

1174

THE BURNING OF "SUBVERSIVE" AND "UN-GERMAN" BOOKS IN 1933

of bringing real socialism to Germany. Although he was rapidly gaining control of the economy of the country, he did not interfere with the profits of the industrialists or break up the holdings of the landowners.

Hitler discovered that Roehm was even doing a little political plotting, trying to win a stronger position for himself in the Nazi government. Conferring with Goering and Himmler, Hitler decided to kill Roehm and his closest followers. This would also be a good opportunity for Hitler to kill some other people who might someday prove troublesome. The job would be done by the SS men and special police under the direction of Goering.

On June 30, 1934, they struck in the "blood purge" that shocked the world. Roehm was thrown into a prison cell and, when he refused to take his own life, was shot by two SS officers. General von Schleicher, a former chancellor of Germany, was shot down in the doorway of his own home, as was his wife. Some of the people who died that day were shot in groups, like the 150 storm troopers who fell before a firing squad in Berlin. Some were shot because they knew too much about Hitler's past. One man was even shot by mistake. He was a Munich music critic named Dr. Willi Schmid. He was killed as he was playing the cello in his study, while his wife and two small children were in the next room.

and girls were forced to join various organizations of the "Hitler Youth." They had no choice. Parents who interfered in any way were imprisoned. When a boy reached the age of ten, he took this oath:

"In the presence of the blood banner, which represents our Fuehrer, I swear to devote all my energies and my strength to the savior of our country, Adolph Hitler. I am willing and ready to give up my life for him, so help me God."

Girls were taught that the chief duty of women was to have children for Nazi Germany. Boys were given military drill and went hiking with rifles and heavy packs. When a boy reached the age of eighteen, he entered the Labor Service or the army. The army was the real center of German life under the Nazis, for Hitler preached that war was the greatest glory of man. And Hitler needed war; he and the Nazis could not survive without it. Only war and conquest could save the German economy.

In time, Germany would attack. Meanwhile, conditions became somewhat better for the German people. It was true that the workers were controlled by Hitler's Labor Front. They had to work where and when they were told. It was also true that, without labor unions, workers had to take whatever pay they were offered. While profits were rising, wages were falling. Still, there were jobs to be had, even if the pay was low. As for civil liberties, Germans had never had much political freedom, except under the Weimar Republic. They felt that, if they had lost their freedom, they had also lost the "freedom to starve."

And so, while their Jewish and anti-Nazi neighbors were dragged off to concentration camps, most Germans were satisfied enough with the Nazis. The shrieks of the tortured and the moans of the dying were drowned out by the tramp of soldiers through the streets, by the shouts of *"Heil Hitler!"*, by the propaganda speeches that poured from loudspeakers, by the wheels of factories busily grinding out instruments of death. Under the flag of the swastika, led by their Fuehrer, the master race was preparing for war.

GERMAN CHILDREN WERE FORCED TO JOIN THE HITLER YOUTH WHICH TRAINED THEM FOR SERVICE IN THE ARMED FORCES.

Dictatorship and a Civil War

1926-1939

THE END OF World War I brought many changes of government in Europe. But in a number of countries the old aristocrats and landowners still had power, and the new governments could not solve the problems that faced them. Among these countries was Poland. A democratic form of government had been established, but conflicts between various parties and their leaders kept it from being very effective.

General Joseph Pilsudski had helped to set up the new government of Poland. He retired from public office in 1922, when Poland adopted a democratic constitution. Pilsudski wanted a bigger and stronger Poland, and he was dissatisfied with what the government was doing. In 1926 he led his armed followers on Warsaw, the nation's capital, and the tramp of marching men sounded in Poland, as it did in Italy and Germany. Within a few days, Pilsudski was in control of the government. Although from time to time he held various offices in the government, Pilsudski was really the dictator of Poland until his death in 1935.

Shortly before he died, Pilsudski put through a new constitution. While it called for certain democratic procedures, such as the election of a parliament, it merely made official Pilsudski's military dictatorship. Pilsudski's place was taken by General Edward Smigly-Rydz, the inspector-general of the army. He ruled with the aid of a group of military men known as the "colonels." Although Poland's political organization was looser than that of Germany or Italy, its form of government was very close to fascism.

Much the same thing was true in the countries of the Balkans—in Greece, Yugoslavia, Albania, Bulgaria, and Rumania. During the 1920's and early 1930's Greece tried various forms of government. It was at times a monarchy, at times a dictatorship, and at times a democratic republic. In 1936, however, King George named General John Metaxas as head of the government. Metaxas did away with elections and the National Assembly, and he ruled as a dictator until 1941.

Yugoslavia was also a monarchy, but Peter II, who became king in 1935, was too young to rule. A regency was set up, headed by Prince Paul Karageorgevich. Although Yugoslavia had a parliament, it was under the control of the regency and the government party.

Albania, Bulgaria, and Rumania were all monarchies in which the king set up a royal dictatorship. In 1939, however, Mussolini drove out Albania's king and took over the rule of that small country. In Rumania, the government was menaced by the Iron Guard, a fascist party which had the support of Nazi Germany.

In Portugal, in the southwest corner of Europe, a military dictatorship took over the government. Beginning in 1928, Antonio de Oliveira Salazar, a university professor, became the most important figure in the country. In 1933, under a new constitution, Salazar set up a strict dictatorship that held Portugal in a firm grip.

But it was Portugal's neighbor, Spain, which attracted the attention of the world. During the years immediately following World War I, Spain had a constitutional monarchy, with King Alfonso on the throne. Socialists and other radicals, however, were beginning to win influence over the people, and there were a number of strikes and riots. To make things even worse, Spain was having trouble in Spanish Morocco, the territory it held in Africa. Troops were sent to that region to put down the native Riffs, who were led by the chieftain Abd-el-Krim. In 1921, the Riffs trapped a Spanish force of 20,000 men, killing 12,000 of them.

Shocked by this disaster, the Spanish people became even more restless. To control them, King Alfonso allowed General Miguel Primo de Rivera to become military dictator in 1923. Rivera was not very successful, and finally, in 1930, he resigned. Although Alfonso promised the people more rights, they had turned against him and refused to be satisfied with promises. Crowds gathered in the streets, shouting, "Down with the king! Down with the monarchy!" A year later, the king was forced to flee, and a republic was established. The new government confiscated property belonging to the aristocrats and the Catholic Church, and put through a number of reforms.

While a majority of the people supported the

FRANCISCO FRANCO

republic, Spain was a divided country. The Socialists, the Communists, and another group of radicals, the syndicalists, all gave support to the republic, but they all demanded further and more drastic reforms. Opposed to the republic was a coalition of aristocrats, landowners, industrialists, monarchists, and much of the hierarchy of the Catholic Church. Also opposed to the republic was the army—and the army took the lead in rebelling against the government.

The rebellion began in Morocco in July of 1936. Most of the army and almost all of its officers rallied to the Nationalists, as the rebels called themselves. One of their leaders was General Francisco Franco, and it was he who would become their head. Soon the rebels were receiving help from Fascist Italy and Nazi Germany —men, arms, ships, and planes.

The Loyalists, as the supporters of the republic were called, quickly organized a militia, and they were able to keep Franco's army from taking Madrid, the capital city. To strengthen the government, Socialists and Communists were added to the cabinet, and a Socialist, Francisco Largo Caballero, became premier. But when the Loyalists asked for help from other nations, they were deeply disappointed. The United States, Britain, and France were afraid that the war might spread to all of Europe. They decided on a policy of "non-intervention"—that is, they refused to help either side. The republic was forced to rely on aid from the Soviet Union, which sold Spain some tanks, planes, and supplies, and sent some officers. Volunteers from many countries, however, rushed to Spain to fight against fascism in the International Brigades. Among them were Americans who fought under Communist leadership in the Abraham Lincoln Brigade.

Nazi Germany saw in the Spanish civil war a good opportunity to test new weapons and methods of killing. In April of 1937, German planes attacked the historic town of Guernica. They dropped bombs on civilians, including a large number of women and children, and destroyed the town. The world—except for the fascists— was horrified. Spain, the romantic land of castles and bullfights, of song and dance, of castanets and guitars, had become the scene of a mass murder—the kind of killing that would be practiced on an even larger scale in World War II.

The people of Spain and the volunteers of the International Brigades fought bravely and well. As the Nationalists pushed on, the Loyalists said, "*No paseran*"—"they shall not pass," and "Madrid will be the grave of fascism." But they were no match for Franco's army, backed by men and guns and tanks and planes from Italy and Germany. Besides, the Russians were using their aid to gain power and wipe out the Trotskyites and anti-Communist Loyalists. In March of 1939, Franco marched into Madrid, and Spain was no longer a republic. At least 700,000 soldiers had been killed, while 30,000 persons had been executed or assassinated, and 15,000 had lost their lives in air raids.

JAPAN EXPANDS

In August of that same year, General Franco proclaimed himself *Caudillo,* or leader, "responsible only to God and to history." Spain became a fascist dictatorship with one party and no civil liberties. The story was much the same as it had been in Italy and Germany, except for one thing. In Germany, Hitler controlled the churches and made Nazism into a sort of religion. In Italy, a strongly Catholic country, Mussolini and the Catholic Church were forced to come uneasily to terms. Spain was even more strongly Catholic than Italy, and Franco made Catholicism the state religion. Anti-Franco Catholics—including many priests—fled into exile.

Meanwhile, in Asia, another country was liv-

A STREET IN GUERNICA, DESTROYED BY GERMAN PLANES

A RAILWAY EXPLOSION SET OFF THE JAPANESE INVASION OF MANCHURIA.

ing under a dictatorship that had most of the features of fascism. With a large and growing population crowded on the four islands of its homeland, Japan had for long been interested in expansion. After its unexpected victory against Russia in 1905, Japan took its place as one of the military powers of the world. Although Japan had an emperor, real control was in the hands of the military men and the *zaibatsu*—the family groups that owned the big businesses and industries. Japan needed more land, and its leaders were especially tempted by the vast territories of China. During the 1920's, however, the *zaibatsu* turned their attention to building up the nation's industry, and democratic ideas began to take hold among the people.

Even so, the militarists remained strong and continued to make plans. In 1927, General Baron Glichi Tanaka was supposed to have sent a report to the emperor which said:

"In the future, if we want to control China, we must first crush the United States just as in the past we had to fight the Russo-Japanese War. But in order to conquer China we must first conquer Manchuria and Mongolia. In order to conquer the world, we must first conquer China. If we succeed in conquering China the rest of the Asian countries and the South Seas countries will fear us and surrender. Then the world will realize that Eastern Asia is ours and will not dare to violate our rights. This is the plan left to us by Emperor Meiji, the success of which is essential to our national existence."

When news of this reached the outside world, the Japanese government stated that no such report had been made. Nevertheless, the events of the following years proved that the militarists did indeed have a plan of conquest. They gained more strength during the great depression of 1929, which ruined Japan's silk industry. To get what they wanted, they even assassinated government officials, and by 1931 they were the greatest power in Japan.

That year, too, they were ready to act on their plan. In September there was an explosion on the railway in Manchuria, near Mukden. The Japanese army charged that Chinese soldiers had set off the explosion, and ordered troops into Mukden. China protested to the League of Nations, but the Japanese refused to abide by the League's decisions and eventually left the League altogether. They drove on into Manchuria, until at last they declared Manchuria and Inner Mongolia independent. They then set up their own state, calling it Manchukuo.

The militarists had now won the support of the *zaibatsu* and were in full control of Japan. For the people, it meant the end of anything resembling democracy. Under the banner of the rising sun, Japan was marching down the road that would lead it to war against China and, later, the United States.

1182

The Meaning of Totalitarianism

AND SO it happened that in many parts of the world people were living under a system of government that came to be called totalitarianism. There were differences in the governments of the totalitarian countries, but they were alike in certain important ways. In each of them, the government was controlled by one political party, usually under a dictator, and no other political parties were allowed. The ruling party was not satisfied to control the government; its aim was total control of the life of its people. It controlled the courts and the armed forces, labor and industry, science and the arts. In some countries, it controlled religion completely; in others, religious groups were allowed to exist so long as they did not challenge the power of the government.

To keep their strict control of the people, the totalitarian governments set up a secret police, and totalitarian countries were often called "police states." The people had no civil liberties and no part in the governing of the country. They had to obey and do as they were told. If they did not, they risked prison, concentration camp, torture, and death.

As totalitarianism spread widely over the world, men began to wonder what had made it possible. The reasons were not too difficult to find. The end of World War I had left many countries, especially those that had been defeated, divided and disorganized. Their weak governments could not solve the problems that faced them. This gave "strong men" the chance to take over the government.

Another important reason was the great depression that began around 1929. Business seemed to come to a standstill. Unsold goods piled up in warehouses, while factories shut down and millions of people were thrown out of work. Hungry people were willing to listen to anyone who promised them food and jobs. Freedom no longer seemed to matter; what good was freedom to a starving man? A dictator might improve conditions; things could hardly get worse. At the same time, the leaders of business and industry were afraid of a revolution that might strip them of their wealth. They supported the parties that promised to save the country—and their profits.

But the totalitarian governments had no real solution for the problems of their countries. They could grow fat only at someone else's expense. To survive, they had to gobble up territory owned by other nations. They had to expand—and expansion, if resisted, meant war. The big exception was the Soviet Union. It, too, was totalitarian, but in the early years after the revolution it was too weak to fight. Besides, it was a vast country with great natural resources. Stalin decided that the first thing Russia must do was build up its industry. Meanwhile, Germany, Italy, and Japan prepared to grab all they could.

The depression also struck the great democracies of the United States, Great Britain, and France. As the depression deepened, the world watched to see what they would do. Could they find a democratic way to solve their problems? Or would they, too, give way to totalitarianism?

A NAZI LEADS PRISONERS MARKED FOR DEATH TO THE GAS CHAMBERS.

Panic in Wall Street

1929-1932

As millions of Americans hurried to work on the morning of October 24, 1929, it seemed like the start of an ordinary day. It seemed just as ordinary to the brokers and bankers who were entering their offices on New York's Wall Street. True, the prices of stocks had been falling for several days, but that was nothing to worry about. There were bound to be ups and downs in the stock market, and prices would surely rise again.

For never before had the United States known such prosperity as it did in the 1920's. Herbert Hoover, who had become President seven months before, had said, "We in America are nearer to the final triumph over poverty than ever before in the history of any land. . . . We have not reached the goal, but given a chance to go forward with the policies of the last eight years, we shall soon with the help of God be in sight of the day when poverty will be banished from this nation."

Many Americans agreed with him. They invested their savings in stocks, and, just as they hoped, the price of stocks rose. To make even more money, they bought stocks on margin—that is, on credit. They knew that they could be wiped out if stocks took a sudden tumble, but why should that happen? The richest men in the country said it wouldn't, and if they didn't know, who did? The country was booming, and anyone who didn't get rich was a fool.

More and more Americans bought stocks, and prices went higher and higher—until October of 1929. As the prices of stocks began to fall, people stopped buying and began to sell. The more they sold, the lower prices fell; the lower prices fell, the more they sold. But there seemed to be no reason to be seriously worried. This had happened before and would happen again. And always, in the past, stocks had bounced back up until they hit new highs. So why worry?

Then suddenly, on Thursday, the twenty-fourth of October, came a surprise—a dreadful

WORRIED INVESTORS CROWDED WALL STREET DURING THE CRASH.

and terrible surprise. No one wanted to buy and everyone wanted to sell. A roar rose from the Stock Exchange in New York as traders tried to keep up with the orders to sell. It was no use; the orders kept pouring in—sell, sell, sell. And prices kept falling—falling lower, and lower, and lower still. The news spread, and crowds gathered in Wall Street and in the offices of brokers everywhere in the city. Men who had yesterday been rich or at least well off stared at one another in disbelief, realizing that their fortunes had been wiped out.

Early that afternoon, the heads of the most important banks in New York met at No. 1 Wall Street, the office of J. P. Morgan and Company. Each put up $40,000,000—$240,000,000 in all—to buy stocks and stop the fall of prices.

1184

They did stop it, but only temporarily, and by November prices had slid down to new lows. And yet, bad as the stock market crash was, worse was in store for the American people. A depression had begun, a great depression that would affect every person in the country. With the end of the 1920's and the beginning of the 1930's, businesses shut up shop, factories closed, prices of goods dropped, profits fell, wages were cut, and millions of workers lost their jobs. By 1931, 7,000,000 people were out of work.

As jobless men tramped from one employment office to another, only to be turned away, they wondered what had happened. What had brought on the end of prosperity? What had changed America almost overnight? Had there been no warning?

Even years later, there would be no agreement on what had actually started the stock market panic. But there had been warning signals about the depression for some time. Farmers were already in trouble during the 1920's. Prices of manufactured goods had risen faster than prices of farm products, and farmers did not have enough money to buy the things they needed. The number of unemployed was around 1,000,000, and it had gone to 1,800,000 in 1928.

Wealth was unevenly distributed. In 1929, 24,000 families had yearly incomes of $100,000, while 42.4 per cent of all American families earned less than $1,500. Workers were producing more per man than they had before 1919, but wages had not gone up enough for them to buy the vast quantity of goods in the stores. And high tariffs on imported goods—passed by Congress against the wishes of President Hoover—meant less trade with Europe. Unable to sell to

FEW BANKERS THOUGHT THAT THE CRASH INDICATED ANY SERIOUS DIFFICULTIES.

WORST STOCK CRASH STEMMED BY BANKS; 12,894,650-SHARE DAY SWAMPS MARKET; LEADERS CONFER, FIND CONDITIONS SOUND

From "The New York Times," October 25, 1929.

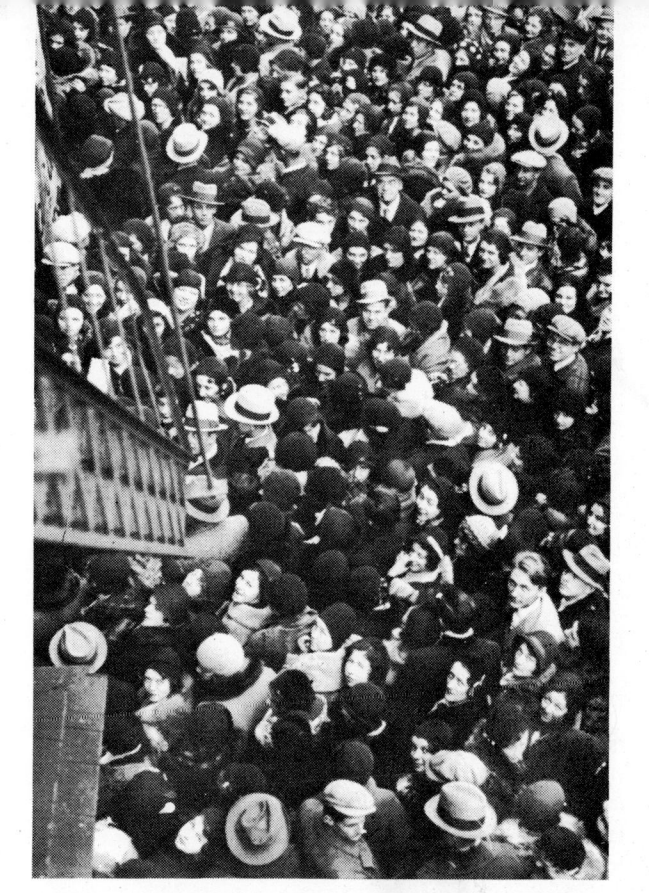

THE UNEMPLOYED RUSHED TO APPLY FOR THE VERY FEW JOBS AVAILABLE.

America, European countries could not pay their debts or buy goods made in America.

While jobless men wondered what had happened in the past, they were worried about the present and fearful of the future. Their chances of getting a job seemed to grow less each day, and each day ate up more of their small savings. What would they and their families do when it was gone? They looked for help to the government, especially to President Hoover. He was known as an able administrator. During and after World War I, he had been in charge of organizations supplying food to the starving people of Europe. Surely he would do as much for Americans.

President Hoover assured the people that the economy of the nation was basically sound, and that it was now suffering from a lack of confidence. Confidence would return, and so would prosperity. In fact, the return of prosperity was just around the corner. And he had no intention of letting people starve.

He said, "This is not an issue as to whether people shall go hungry or cold in the United States. It is solely a question of the best method

SHANTYTOWNS OR "HOOVERVILLES" SPRANG UP ON THE OUTSKIRTS OF CITIES.

by which hunger and cold shall be prevented. It is a question as to whether the American people, on the one hand, will maintain the spirit of charity and mutual self-help through voluntary giving and the responsibility of local government as distinguished, on the other hand, from appropriations out of the Federal Treasury for such purposes. . . . I am willing to pledge myself that if the time should ever come that the voluntary agencies of the country, together with local and State governments, are unable to find resources with which to prevent hunger and suffering in my country, I will ask the aid of every resource of the Federal Government because I would no more see starvation amongst our countrymen than would any Senator or Congressman. I have faith in the American people that such a day will not come."

HOOVER AND THE DEPRESSION

Hoover wanted to avoid using Federal money for direct relief unless it was absolutely necessary; he believed this was best for the country and for the people. He did, however, take action in other directions. He called in the heads of large industries and tried to persuade them to cut wages as little as possible. To raise the price of farm products and help the farmer, he set up agencies that bought up surplus wheat and cotton. To help business, he set up the Reconstruction Finance Corporation, which loaned money to businesses such as railroads, banks, and insurance and utility companies. To create jobs, he spent millions of dollars—more than any President before him—on the construction of roads and public buildings, and for the improvement of rivers and harbors. Hoover also tried to help the European nations that were having difficulty paying their debts to the United States. He arranged a one-year moratorium on their payments—that is, for one year they would not have to pay anything.

The Reconstruction Finance Corporation saved many businesses from going bankrupt, and would be continued in future administrations. But, with conditions so bad, industry could not keep wages up. The farm program failed to raise the price of farm products. The construction program failed to create enough jobs. In spite of everything Hoover did, the depression grew worse, and by 1932 the number of unemployed was about 12,000,000.

Men sold apples at five cents apiece on street corners, trying to earn a few pennies. Others walked the streets, begging from passersby, or stood in breadlines to get something to eat. Little villages of shacks, made of packing cases and scrap wood and metal, sprang up on the outskirts of cities. They were called "Hoovervilles," a bitter joke at the expense of the President many Americans felt was not doing enough to help them.

Thousands of men, as well as boys in their teens, hopped freight trains and traveled the country, hoping that things would be better in the next town. Farmers who could not pay their debts were losing their farms. Home-owners who could not meet their payments were losing their houses. Families that could not pay their rent were put out on the streets. Sometimes children even searched through garbage cans, hoping to find something fit to eat.

In June of 1932, more than 15,000 veterans of World War I streamed into Washington to urge Congress to give veterans a bonus. Some of them brought their wives and children, and they camped near the city or on vacant lots near the Capitol. When Congress voted against the bonus, most of them left. But several thousand remained and Hoover ordered them ousted. Troops, led by General Douglas MacArthur, drove them out with tanks, tear gas, and bayonets. The

THE "BONUS ARMY" WAS DRIVEN AWAY AFTER IT MET ON THE CAPITOL STEPS.

incident of the "Bonus Army" added to Hoover's unpopularity, but the Republicans could find no one better to run for president in 1932. He easily won the nomination. The Democrats nominated Franklin Delano Roosevelt.

UNEMPLOYED MEN AND WOMEN SELLING APPLES BECAME A FAMILIAR SIGHT.

FRANKLIN DELANO ROOSEVELT

The New Deal

1933

WHEN Franklin Delano Roosevelt was nominated in 1932, he was fifty years old. A fifth cousin of former President Theodore Roosevelt, he came of a wealthy family. He grew up on a large estate at Hyde Park, New York, overlooking the Hudson River. At the age of twenty-four he married Eleanor Roosevelt, a distant cousin and a niece of Theodore Roosevelt. Several years after graduating from Harvard and studying law at Columbia University, he entered politics and was elected to the state senate. In the presidential campaign of 1912 he supported Woodrow Wilson, who named him assistant secretary of the Navy. In 1920, Roosevelt ran for vice president, but he and his running-mate, James M. Cox, lost the election to Warren G. Harding and Calvin Coolidge.

Even so, Roosevelt had become nationally known, and it looked as though he had a bright future in politics. Then, less than a year later, while on vacation, he fell ill of poliomyelitis. At first he was paralyzed from the waist down, but slowly, painfully, he fought his way back to health. He would never be able to walk normally, and he would be forced to use a wheelchair most of the time. But he learned to get about with the aid of braces on his legs, leaning on canes or crutches. In 1924 he made his first public appearance since his illness. He hobbled on crutches to the speaker's platform at Madison Square Garden in New York, where he placed Alfred E. Smith's name in nomination before the Democratic presidential convention. The cheers of the audience were as much for Roosevelt as they were for Smith.

HAPPY DAYS ARE HERE AGAIN

Roosevelt's battle against illness had left him a changed man. Francis Perkins, who later became his Secretary of Labor, said that he "emerged completely warmhearted, with humility of spirit and with a deeper philosophy. Having been in the depths of trouble, he understood the problems of people in trouble. Although he rarely, almost never, spoke of his illness in later years, he showed that he had developed faith in the capacity of troubled people to respond to help and encouragement."

Roosevelt was still not sure, however, that he would return to politics. In 1928, when he was asked to run for governor of New York, he replied, "I'm not well enough to run. It's out of the question." But when Alfred E. Smith told him that the Democrats could not win without him, he changed his mind and campaigned vigorously. He was elected, served two terms, and in the hot July of 1932 was nominated for President. Then he did something no candidate had ever done. He traveled by plane to Chicago to give his speech of acceptance before the convention. In the speech, he said, "I pledge you, I pledge myself, to a new deal for the American people."

A new deal.... The American people liked the sound of those words. They seemed to offer hope, a promise of action and better times to come. And, indeed, Roosevelt was already show-

A Changing Nation

was unconstitutional, and the proud Blue Eagle was a dead bird. What was shocking was not so much the fact that the NRA had been killed; after all, it had been a disappointment. But the Court's decision made it appear as if no Federal law could be passed to regulate wages, hours, or other procedures in industry. Roosevelt called it "more important probably than any decision since the Dred Scott case." He said that the big issue was: "Does this decision mean that the United States government has no control over any economic problem?"

Although this was a serious setback, the New Deal went on. Roosevelt kept experimenting and planning, changing his plans when necessary, doing what he thought best to beat the depression and bring reforms to the nation. In 1935 he set up the Works Progress Administration, or WPA. People on relief were given jobs and paid out of Federal money. They were put to work building and improving roads, bridges, parks, schools, hospitals, and sewage and water systems. Professional people, including artists, writers, actors, and musicians, were also given jobs. Writers wrote reports, histories of various regions, and guidebooks of the states. Artists painted pictures and did murals in postoffices and other public buildings. Musicians gave concerts, and actors put on plays at low admission prices as part of the Federal Theater Project. To help young people between the ages of sixteen and twenty-five, the National Youth Administration was set up. It provided part-time work, so that students could continue to attend high schools and colleges.

That same year, Congress passed a bill increasing taxes on high incomes. It also passed the Public Utility Security Act, which regulated certain financial practices by electric power companies. Most important of all, it passed the Social Security Act, which would affect millions of Americans for years to come. Under this act, workers who retired at the age of sixty-five were to receive monthly payments for the rest of their lives. The amount would depend on how much they had earned during their working years. The money was to come from a special tax, half paid by workers, half by employers. The act also provided for pensions for the disabled and for the poor over the age of sixty-five, for benefits to wid-

FARMERS FLED THE DUST BOWL TO SEEK WORK IN CALIFORNIA.

ows and children, and for unemployment insurance, which allowed anyone who lost his job to collect benefits for about fifteen weeks.

When the Supreme Court outlawed the NRA, it had, of course, outlawed Section 7a, which gave workers the right to join unions without interference from employers. With the rise in union membership, labor had become more powerful in politics. Now labor leaders demanded something to take the place of Section 7a, and on July 5, 1935, Congress passed the National Labor Relations Act. This act was often called the Wagner Act, after Senator Robert F. Wagner of New York, who led the battle to get it passed. Similar to Section 7a, it set up the National Labor Relations Board. The board was to supervise elections among workers in plants and industries so that they could be represented by the unions they wanted, or not represented at all.

Encouraged by the new law, more thousands of workers joined unions. And yet, even as labor was growing in strength and power, it was divided. Most of the unions were part of the American Federation of Labor, or A.F. of L., which followed the policy of organizing workers in craft unions. There was one union for all carpenters, another for all bricklayers, another for all coal miners, and so on. Some union leaders said this was an old-fashioned method. They wanted industrial unions—unions which would take in all workers in a particular industry, no matter what job they did.

JOHN L. LEWIS

Among the supporters of industrial unions was bushy-browed John L. Lewis, head of the United Mine Workers. William L. Hutcheson, president of the Carpenters' Union, disagreed with him, and the two went at it with their fists at the A.F. of L. convention in 1935. That October, Lewis and the heads of seven other unions formed the Committee for Industrial Organization, which became known as the C.I.O., to work for industrial unions.

One of the unions allied with the C.I.O. was the United Automobile Workers, and in December of 1936 it went on strike against Chrysler Motors and the mighty General Motors Corporation. The union tried something that had seldom been tried before in the United States—a "sit-down" strike. Instead of picketing, the workers stayed in the plants, so that strike breakers could not come in and do their jobs. Food was brought to them from kitchens set up by the union.

The sit-down was, technically, illegal, and the companies were determined not to settle with the union. The strikers were just as determined. They were angry at the frequent lay-offs, and the fast pace of the assembly line. It had not been easy for them to organize, and they angrily accused the companies of spending large sums of money to hire detectives to spy on them and of finding some excuse to fire any man suspected of joining the union. And so the strikers sat it out, while the companies tried to get at them through the courts, and the Federal and state governments tried to find a way to reach a peaceful settlement.

Whether the sit-down was or was not legal, the strikers had taken their stand and it was up to the companies to get them out. The police took a hand on January 11, 1937, when they rushed a plant in Flint, Michigan. They used tear gas and buckshot, and the strikers fought back with pop bottles, pieces of pipe, and anything else they could pick up. The strikers won that battle, and the sit-down went on. Then the courts ordered them to get out, and soldiers of the National Guard were to see that they did. The deadline was the afternoon of February 3, which was a freezing cold day. Thousands of union men gathered to stop the soldiers, and there was danger of violence. But, before any fighting could break out, the men were cheering and dancing in the streets. News had come that General Motors was at last willing to meet with the union leaders. A week later, the company agreed

STRIKERS AND POLICE CLASH IN 1937.

to recognize the union and, after 44 days, the strike was over.

In March came an even greater surprise. The C.I.O. had been trying to organize the workers of the United States Steel Corporation, which labor had always considered one of the toughest foes. But John L. Lewis of the C.I.O. had been quietly meeting with Myron C. Taylor, the steel company's chairman of the board, and they had worked out an agreement under which the company would sign a contract with the C.I.O. The United States Steel Corporation was "Big Steel," the largest company in the industry. The smaller companies, known as "Little Steel," refused to follow its lead and would not sign with the union until 1941. Meanwhile there were strikes and violence. On May 30, 1937, Memorial Day, ten workers were killed by the police at the Republic Steel plant in South Chicago, Illinois.

In spite of the difficulties with Little Steel, union membership kept rising. Weak and insignificant for so many years, unions became a familiar part of American life. But labor continued to be divided, and became more so in 1938. The A.F. of L. supended the unions in the C.I.O., which then became an independent group under the name of the Congress of Industrial Organizations.

The Election of 1936
1936

As Roosevelt's first term in office neared its end, many people in the United States—and in other countries—wondered if the New Deal could really solve America's problems. More than that, they wondered if Americans would continue to follow the path of democracy. A wave of totalitarianism was sweeping the world; would it reach as far as America?

1195

AMERICANS OF THE DEPRESSION DAYS WAITING TO CAST THEIR VOTES

Many American intellectuals—scientists, teachers, writers, painters, actors—supported the Communists. They feared the spread of fascism, and it seemed to them that the Communists had taken the lead in the fight against fascism. And with the world in the grip of a great depression, it looked as though Karl Marx's predictions were coming true. Capitalism had indeed failed, fascism was a terrible menace, and communism was the only hope of the world. Millions of people were jobless, but in the Soviet Union there was no unemployment. When it was pointed out to them that there was also no freedom in the Soviet Union, they replied that only under communism could the people be truly free, or that the Soviet Union was surrounded by enemies and could not yet afford to give its people freedom.

With the Roosevelt administration under attack from the right and the left, the world waited to see what would happen. But, as Roosevelt pushed through his New Deal reforms, democracy proved to have great strength. The passing of the Social Security Act left the Townsendites without a real cause to fight for. In September of 1935, Huey Long was shot and killed, for personal reasons, by a young Louisiana doctor. The leaders of the Catholic Church showed that they did not approve of Father Coughlin, who was beginning to sound more and more anti-Semitic, and he began to lose his following.

As for the Communists, they had never been able to attract a large number of Americans. Then Stalin, through the Communist International, ordered all Communists to form "united fronts" with liberals and all groups opposed to fascism. The American Communists threw their support to Roosevelt and the New Deal. Earl Browder, the head of the party, went so far as to say that "Communism is twentieth-century Americanism."

But the big test for Roosevelt was yet to come —the election of 1936. Roosevelt himself was confident of victory. In November of 1935, he said, "We will win easily next year." And then he added, "But we are going to make it a crusade." Political observers, however, believed it was not at all certain that he would win. A number of prominent Democrats had turned against him. Among them was Al Smith, whom Roosevelt himself had once nominated for president.

Many men of wealth and position supported Roosevelt and felt that his reforms would save the existing system, but others bitterly opposed him. They called him "that man in the White House" and told stories about him, about his wife, about his sons. He was practically a com-

The Election of 1936

munist and wanted to make himself dictator. He had raised taxes and was spending the money hand over fist. He was making Americans soft; why should they work when they could get handouts from the government? Why, even long-haired artists, writers, musicians, actors, and dancers were living off the government! Meanwhile, businessmen were having a harder and harder time. Each day there were more government regulations, more government interference. Roosevelt had brought socialism to America. He was out to "soak the rich." He was ruining them. He was ruining the country. Conservative newspapers echoed these remarks, and kept attacking Roosevelt and his policies. A group of wealthy men formed an organization, the Liberty League, to fight Roosevelt and the New Deal.

Roosevelt was nominated by the Democrats without opposition, and immediately began his "crusade." In his speech accepting the nomination, he called his opponents "economic royalists." He said that they "complain that we seek to overthrow the institutions of America. What they really complain of is that we seek to overthrow their power."

The Republicans nominated Alfred M. Landon, the governor of Kansas. The Communists and the Socialists also ran candidates, and there was a new party in the field—the Union party. This was made up of followers of Coughlin, Townsend, and Huey Long, and it nominated William Lemke. The campaign was a bitter one, but when the election returns were in, they proved that Roosevelt's prediction had been right. He had won easily.

Even Roosevelt, however, could not have expected so great a victory. He carried every state except Maine and Vermont. He received 27,751,000 votes, while Landon received 16,679,000. The other candidates trailed far behind. Lemke got 882,000 votes, the Socialists 187,000, and the Communists 80,000.

PRESIDENT AND MRS. ROOSEVELT TOURED THE COUNTRY IN THE 1936 CAMPAIGN.

The Election of 1936

LANDON, 1,293,669; ROOSEVELT, 972,897

Final Returns in The Digest's Poll of Ten Million Voters

Well, the great battle of the ballots in the Poll of ten million voters, scattered throughout the forty-eight States of the Union, is now finished, and in the table below we record the figures received up to the hour of going to press.

These figures are exactly as received from more than one in every five voters polled in our country—they are neither weighted, adjusted nor interpreted.

Never before in an experience covering more than a quarter of a century in taking polls have we received so many different lican National Committee purchased THE LITERARY DIGEST?" And all types and varieties, including: "Have the Jews purchased THE LITERARY DIGEST?" "Is the Pope of Rome a stockholder of THE LITERARY DIGEST?" And so it goes—all equally absurd and amusing. We could add more to this list, and yet all of these questions in recent days are but repetitions of what we have been experiencing all down the years from the very first Poll.

Problem—Now, are the figures in this Poll correct? In answer to this question we will returned and let the people of the Nation draw their conclusions as to our accuracy. So far, we have been right in every Poll. Will we be right in the current Poll? That, as Mrs. Roosevelt said concerning the President's reelection, is in the 'lap of the gods.'

"We never make any claims before election but we respectfully refer you to the opinion of one of the most quoted citizens to-day, the Hon. James A. Farley, Chairman of the Democratic National Committee. This is what Mr. Farley said October 14, 1932:

"Any sane person can not escape the implication of such a gigantic sampling of popular opinion as is embraced in THE LITERARY DIGEST straw vote. I consider this conclusive evidence as to the desire of the

THE *LITERARY DIGEST* WENT OUT OF BUSINESS AFTER THIS INCORRECT PREDICTION.

What had given Roosevelt such a tremendous victory? Landon was far from being the fascist that the Communists called him; in fact, he was something of a liberal. But he had been supported by the Liberty League, and the people had thought of him as the millionaire's candidate. Roosevelt, on the other hand, had seemed to be the candidate of the common man, and had won the votes of labor and the big cities.

Roosevelt Battles the Court
1937-1939

BEGINNING his second term, Roosevelt made it plain that the New Deal would go on. He would continue to work for reforms. He said in his second inaugural address:

"In this nation I see tens of millions of its citizens—a substantial part of its whole population—who at this very moment are denied the greater part of what the very lowest standards of today call the necessities of life.

"I see millions of families trying to live on incomes so meager that the pall of family disaster hangs over them.

"I see millions whose daily lives in city and on farm continue under conditions labelled indecent by so-called polite society of half a century ago.

"I see millions denied education, recreation, and the opportunity to better their lot and that of their children.

"I see millions lacking the means to buy the products of farm and factory and by their poverty denying work and productiveness to many other millions.

"I see one-third of a nation ill-housed, ill-clad, ill-nourished. . . .

"It is not in despair that I paint for you that picture. I paint it for you in hope, because the nation, seeing and understanding the injustice in it, proposes to paint it out. We are determined to make every American citizen the subject of this country's interest and concern, and we will never regard any faithful law-abiding group within our borders as superfluous. The test of our progress is not whether we add more to the abundance of those who have much, it is whether we provide enough for those who have too little. . . ."

DEFEAT IN THE SENATE

To put through new reforms, Roosevelt felt that something had to be done about the Supreme Court. It had already blocked the NRA and other important New Deal legislation; he was determined not to let that happen again. He cast about for a way to reform the Court, and on February 5, 1937, he announced his plan. Only a few men in his administration had known

Roosevelt Battles the Court

about it, and the announcement was a complete surprise. The plan called for appointing a new judge for every judge who had reached the age of seventy and had not retired. Although the plan was to affect all Federal courts, there could be no doubt that Roosevelt had the Supreme Court in mind. Six of the Court's judges were at least seventy years old. If Roosevelt's plan became law, he would be able to appoint six new judges. The Supreme Court would no longer be made up of "nine old men," as they had been called. Instead, there would be fifteen judges. Six of them would be new, younger men who would see the law in a different way.

Roosevelt's plan was a shock, even to many of his supporters. They agreed that something had to be done about the Court, but they felt that Roosevelt was going about it in an underhanded way. Roosevelt's opponents charged that the plan was an attempt to "pack the Court," and a battle began in Congress. Democratic party leaders were having a hard time lining up votes for the bill, and public opinion seemed to be against it. Nevertheless, Roosevelt insisted that the bill be passed, and the fight went on. When it came to a vote in the Senate, on July 22, it was defeated, 70 to 20.

Meanwhile, something unexpected had happened. The Supreme Court had suddenly begun to approve New Deal legislation. It upheld a number of laws, including the National Labor Relations Act and the Social Security Act. Then Justice Van Devanter, one of the "nine old men," resigned. In August, Roosevelt appointed Senator Hugo L. Black of Alabama to take Van Devanter's place—and again he ran into trouble.

As a senator, Black had been a strong supporter of the New Deal and had been known as a liberal. Now a newspaper reporter dug up proof that once, many years ago, Black had been a member of the Ku Klux Klan. In a radio broadcast, Black admitted that he had been a member of the Klan, but had resigned and never rejoined. He said that he had "no sympathy whatever with any organization or group which, anywhere or at any time, arrogates to itself the

THE SUPREME COURT IN 1937. IT BLOCKED SOME OF ROOSEVELT'S LEGISLATION, BUT HIS PLAN TO REMODEL THE COURT WAS WIDELY OPPOSED.

MANY PEOPLE OPPOSED HUGO BLACK'S APPOINTMENT TO THE SUPREME COURT.

un-American power to interfere in the slightest degree with complete religious freedom." The Senate approved his appointment, and Black became one of the most liberal judges of the Supreme Court. During the next few years, two more judges resigned, and one died. Roosevelt appointed three new men in their place, and never again did he have trouble with the Court. He had lost the battle, but he had won his point.

As it turned out, Roosevelt had lost something more than the battle over the Court. The fight had weakened the Democratic party and his hold on it. The greatest days of the New Deal were coming to an end. Even so, Congress passed several important New Deal bills. Among them was the Wagner-Steagal Housing Act. This set up the United States Housing Authority, which could lend money to cities and states to clear slums and build low-cost housing. Another important bill was the Fair Labor Standards Act, which became law in 1938. It established a minimum wage and a maximum work-week for employees of firms that did business in more than one state. Within three years, the minimum wage was to be raised to forty cents an hour, and the work-week lowered to forty hours. Workers were to be paid time-and-a-half for overtime. Children under sixteen years of age could not be employed, and anyone under eighteen could not be employed at dangerous work.

In 1939, Roosevelt himself said, "We have now passed the period of internal conflict in the launching of our program of social reform. Our full energies may now be released to invigorate the processes of recovery in order to preserve our reforms."

"WAR IS A CONTAGION"

Looking back over the past few years, Americans tried to judge the accomplishments of the New Deal. Roosevelt's first administration, especially the dramatic first hundred days, had been a time of emergency and recovery measures. Then had come a period of reforms. The New Deal had cost a great deal of money, and it had not really pulled America out of the depression. Millions of people were still out of work. But when Roosevelt had taken office, the country had been close to collapse. Somehow he had kept the economy going, and had brought help and hope to the people. Laws had been passed that would have an effect for years to come. Never again would it be possible to say that the government had no responsibility for the welfare of the people. Most important of all, the United States had not gone either fascist or communist. In an age when totalitarianism was spreading, the nation had remained a democracy.

That democracy now faced another danger. As early as 1937, Roosevelt had said, "The peace, the freedom and the security of ninety per cent of the population of the world is being jeopardized by the remaining ten per cent. It seems to be unfortunately true that the epidemic of world lawlessness is spreading. When an epidemic of physical disease starts to spread, the community approves and joins in a quarantine. . . . War is a contagion, whether it be declared or undeclared. . . . We are determined to keep out of war, yet we cannot insure ourselves against the disastrous effects of war and the dangers of involvement."

Before long, what happened in America would be determined by what happened in distant lands, in Europe and in Asia.

"On the Dole"

1918-1936

IN Europe as in America, the leading democratic nations—Great Britain and France—faced the problems of the great depression. In those nations, too, the question arose: Could democracy survive, or would it give way to totalitarianism? Would the people turn instead to fascism or communism?

Although Britain had a brief period of prosperity immediately after World War I, of all the world's democracies, it was struck hardest and soonest by the depression. For Britain had a special problem. A highly industrialized country, it lived by its exports. It sold manufactured goods and coal to other countries, and imported its food.

Even before the war, Britain had begun to lose its markets. Other countries were making wool and cotton cloth, which was one of Britain's most important exports. New fuels were developed that were replacing coal. More and more countries were using high tariffs to keep out foreign goods. After 1918, the situation became even worse. The fact that Britain had long been an industrial country was now working against it. Its machinery and manufacturing methods were old-fashioned and could not compete with the modern machinery and methods of other lands. Exports fell, factories shut down, and millions of Britons were out of work.

Britain had had unemployment insurance as early as 1911. Now the payments were increased, and the unemployed went "on the dole," as they called it. The government also provided old-age pensions, and some medical and housing aid. But the people felt that the unemployment and other benefits were too small, and they were dissatisfied. They began to turn to the Labor party. Up to this time, Britain's strongest political

A DEMONSTRATION OF UNEMPLOYED ARMY VETERANS IN ENGLAND

"On the Dole"

parties had been the Conservative party and the Liberal party, with the Labor party a poor third. In 1922, the Labor party became second only to the Conservatives. Two years later it was elected and Britain had its first Labor government. Ramsay MacDonald was named prime minister.

The Labor party had been formed in 1900 by trade unionists and socialists. It stood for the establishment of socialism, but gradually and by democratic means. It was far from the revolutionary parties of other countries and nothing at all like the Communist party of the Soviet Union. Once in power, the Laborites made no attempt to establish socialism. They recognized the government of the Soviet Union and negotiated several treaties in the hope that the Russians would buy British goods. They extended unemployment insurance, started public works projects, and gave more aid to housing.

Because of their small majority in Parliament, these mild measures were the best they could do for the unemployed. Then the newspapers published a letter that was supposed to have been sent by the Communist International to British labor groups, instructing them to prepare for a revolution. The letter was later proved to be a forgery, but when it was first published it frightened many Englishmen. After all, the Laborites were for socialism, and socialism was the next thing to communism, and Britain wanted none of that. By 1924 the Laborites were voted out and the Conservatives were in.

For five years the Conservatives controlled the government. Stanley Baldwin occupied No. 10 Downing Street—the house in London which was always reserved for the prime minister. The Conservatives placed tariffs on certain goods, but this did little to improve trade and business.

DURING THE 1926 GENERAL STRIKE, WEALTHY VOLUNTEERS TRANSPORTED FOOD AND PEOPLE IN THEIR PRIVATE CARS.

"On the Dole"

The coal mines, particularly, were in trouble, and the price of coal kept falling. When the mine owners tried to cut wages and increase the working day from seven to eight hours, the miners went on strike.

In May of 1926, a number of other trade unions went on strike in support of the miners. Although the strike was called a "general strike," and transportation and other important industries were tied up, no more than half of Britain's 6,000,000 organized workers walked out. Declaring a state of emergency, the government called for volunteers to operate essential services —and got them. In nine days, the general strike was over. The miners remained out for more than seven months, but in the end they were forced to accept the owners' terms.

The following year, the Conservatives passed laws making general strikes illegal and restricting unions in a number of ways. They also passed laws providing for pensions for workers who had reached the age of sixty-five, and pensions for the widows and orphans of workers who died before the retirement age. But business conditions grew worse instead of better, and unemployment rose throughout 1928.

As Britain prepared for the general election of 1929, the Liberal party called for a vast program of public works to end unemployment. The Labor party went much further. It called for the nationalization—that is, government ownership—of certain industries, much higher taxes on the rich, and other drastic reforms. The Conservatives proclaimed that they were the only party that could stop socialism and put the nation's economy on a sound basis.

The election returned the Labor party to power, and again Ramsay MacDonald was prime minister. But again the Laborites had not won enough seats in Parliament for a majority. They were able to put through a few of the things they had promised during the election campaign, but not the sweeping reforms their followers wanted. For now the world-wide depression had struck with full force, and by 1931 Britain had 2,600,000 unemployed. As more and more people went on the dole, the government kept putting more and more money into the unemployment insurance fund. At the same time, it was receiving less and less in taxes. The result was that the nation was deeply in debt, and its financial situation was serious. A committee of experts

"THE DEAD REMEMBERED, THE LIVING FORGOTTEN."

recommended that the government cut down on spending to save the country from financial ruin. This meant lower dole payments, lower pensions, lower salaries, and fewer social services. MacDonald decided to follow the committee's recommendations, and the Labor party split wide open.

Most Laborites were deeply shocked. They remembered that MacDonald had been one of the founders of the Labor party. Born to a poor family in Scotland, as a young man he had come to London, where he became a socialist. He was also a pacifist. When World War I broke out, he took a firm stand against it, even though this made him unpopular for a time. Then he worked his way up to leading positions in the Labor party, and was considered a true representative of the working class. Now he was calling for measures, such as a cut in the dole, that would hit hardest at the workers. He was betraying them and his party; he was betraying his principles; he was a traitor. He and the ministers who supported him were expelled from the Labor party.

The Laborites could no longer stay in power, and MacDonald organized a new government. Called the national government, it was a coalition of members of Britain's three parties. One of the first things it did was to take Britain off the gold standard. In the election of 1931, the National government won an overwhelming victory. Although the Conservatives were by far the strongest party in Parliament, MacDonald continued as prime minister. The National government was successful in balancing the budget, and in time it raised dole payments somewhat. Like the New Deal in the United States, it was unable to solve all the problems of the depression. But the nation did not collapse, and there was never any danger of Britain going communist or fascist. Britain's Communist party was small. Britain had its own Fascist party, but it, too, never attracted many members and had little influence.

In 1935, Ramsay MacDonald resigned and Stanley Baldwin, a Conservative, moved back to No. 10 Downing Street. A year later, King George V died, and the Prince of Wales took the throne as Edward VIII. When Baldwin and his ministers refused to approve Edward's marriage to an American woman who had been twice divorced, Edward gave up the throne to King George VI. Parliament, acting through its ministers, had shown once again that it was the real power in the British government.

An even more important event had taken place in 1931. That year, Parliament approved the Statute of Westminster. It made the dominions—Canada, Australia, New Zealand, and the Union of South Africa—legally equal to Great Britain, and they could govern themselves as they chose. No law passed by their parliaments could be set aside by Great Britain, even if it conflicted with a law passed by the British Parliament. The British Empire had become the British Commonwealth of Nations, and Great Britain was not the head of it, but merely a member, along with the dominions.

During the depression years, Britain not only followed its long tradition of democracy, but strengthened it. Before many years would pass, Britons would be fighting and dying to preserve it.

Democratic But Divided
1926-1939

UNLIKE Britain, France was not a highly industrialized country; its economy was fairly evenly divided between industry and farming. For this reason, the depression came to France later than it did to any of the democracies, and its effect was less severe. But in no other democracy did communists and fascists play so large a part. For a time there was real danger that the French republic would be overthrown by the fascists, and there were riots in the streets.

One reason the fascists were so dangerous was that the French people were sharply divided in their political opinions. There were many parties of many political shades. The largest and most important was the Radical Socialist party, which was neither radical nor socialist. The name was something that had been left over from the past. It was a middle-of-the-road party, supported by the middle class and the farmers.

To the left of the Radical Socialists were the Socialists, who had considerable strength, and the Communists. On the extreme right were the anti-republic parties and the fascists. The most powerful of these was the *Croix de Feu*, the Cross of Fire. Made up mainly of war veterans, it was led by Colonel François de la Rocque, and it won the support of a number of industrialists and financiers. Less strong, though still troublesome, were *Action Française, Camelots du Roi, Solidarité Française, Jeunesse Patriote,* and the *Cagoulards*.

Because of the number of parties, it was almost impossible for any one party to win a majority and control the government. France was governed by coalitions, or combinations, of two or more parties, which supported the premier, the head of the government. But disagreements often arose, and the parties were quick to withdraw their support of the premier. Whenever that happened, a new coalition had to be formed—and it happened often. The result was that the government frequently changed hands, and France had one premier after another. French politics resembled a merry-go-round, whirling at dizzying speed while the riders kept changing horses.

SCANDALS AND RIOTS

When World War I ended, much of northern France was in ruins. Factories, mines, railroads, houses, and farms had been destroyed. In many places, the earth itself had been torn and churned up by artillery shells. Frenchmen felt that they had two main problems—to rebuild their country and to make Germany pay for the damage it had done. Furthermore, they still feared the might of the Germans, and they wanted to prevent them from attacking again in the future.

In 1926, France had serious financial difficulties. Then a so-called National Union government was formed, under Raymond Poincaré, who was known as the "strong man" of France. For several years there was prosperity, but in the 1930's the depression reached France—and with the depression came trouble.

The trouble was set off by a financial and political scandal in 1934. A man named Alexander Stavisky had sold worthless bonds to a number of Frenchmen, cheating them of 200,000,000 francs. He fled to avoid arrest, and then killed himself. A rumor spread that he had been killed by the police to keep him from revealing his connections with people in the government. Newspapers attacked the government, and Camille Chautemps, the premier, was replaced by Édouard Daladier.

Fascist-minded men saw that this was a good chance to strike at the republic, and they staged a huge demonstration against the government in the Place de la Concorde in Paris. Socialists and communists also turned out, to stop the fascists, and Daladier called out a large number of armed soldiers and police. The demonstration took place at night, on February 6, 1934. Fighting had already started between the police and the crowds when, suddenly, the street lights went out. Confused in the darkness, the police and the soldiers fired their guns. Eighteen persons were killed and more than 2,000 were injured.

In the months that followed, one premier took office after another, there was rioting in the streets, and the government ordered two of the fascist groups dissolved. France appeared to be

VETERANS OF WORLD WAR I MARCHED IN PARIS IN 1934.

LÉON BLUM

FASCIST SUPPORTERS BATTLING POLICE ON THE PLACE DE LA CONCORDE

on the verge of revolution and civil war. It seemed that half of the people feared an uprising by the fascists, while the other half feared an uprising by the communists. But, apparently, more people feared fascism. The Radical Socialists, the Socialists, and the Communists decided to unite against the fascists and form the Popular Front. In the election held in the spring of 1936, the Popular Front won a clear-cut victory. For the first time in the nation's history, the Socialists were the strongest party in the Chamber of Deputies, France's most important legislative body. Léon Blum, a prominent Socialist, became premier. The Communists, who had also made gains in the election, refused to take part in the cabinet, but promised to support Blum.

As the Popular Front government took office, a wave of sit-down strikes was sweeping the nation. France's workers were demanding higher pay, a forty-hour work week, and collective bargaining. Blum succeeded in settling the dispute over wages, and industrial firms agreed to give

FRENCH WORKERS DANCING DURING A SIT-DOWN STRIKE IN 1936

the workers higher pay. Laws were passed providing for collective bargaining, the forty-hour week, and paid vacations. The government was also given the right to arbitrate disputes between employers and employees.

THE POPULAR FRONT

Blum made no secret of the fact that he was attempting to do in France what Roosevelt's New Deal was doing in the United States. Reforms were made in the organization of the Bank of France, and steps were taken to bring the armaments and aviation industries under government control. To aid farmers, the price of wheat was fixed. Armed fascist organizations were ordered to disband.

Seldom, if ever, had a French government done so much and so efficiently, and in so short a time. But Blum was not only a Socialist, which conservatives resented; he was a Jew, which led to attacks by the French fascists, who said he was opening the way to a Bolshevik revolution. When Blum asked for emergency powers to deal with financial matters—the same powers which had been given Poincaré ten years before—the Chamber of Deputies agreed. But the Senate refused, and Blum was forced to resign one year after he had taken office.

By 1938, the Popular Front was all but dead. The Radical Socialists alone controlled the government, and Édouard Daladier was again premier. In 1938, the French workers lost the forty-hour week. The government broke their general strike and took further steps against them.

France was still a democracy, but a democracy divided against itself. That division would cost the French dearly in the war that was soon to come.

Totalitarianism Versus Democracy

As the 1930's drew to a close, only eight countries in Europe, besides Great Britain and France, were still democracies. They were Belgium, Holland, Switzerland, Czechoslovakia, Norway, Sweden, Denmark, and Finland. Three of Europe's most important nations were dictatorships. The Soviet Union was communist; Germany and Italy were fascist. There had been dictatorships before, but these went further; they were totalitarian. The word "totalitarian" comes from the word "total," and total control is what these dictatorships were after—total control of their people, total control of their actions and thought.

There were differences between the totalitarian countries. While Stalin exterminated his opponents as ruthlessly as the fascists, he sought to spread his power less by war than by internal revolt. Nor did the Soviets openly preach racial war and genocide. In Germany, however, the Nazis loudly boasted that the Germans were the master race, destined to conquer all other, inferior, peoples. "Today Germany," they said, "tomorrow the world."

Furthermore, the fascists claimed to be the only ones who could stop Communism, and the communists considered the fascists their worst enemies. As a result, the communists in some countries found themselves lined up with the defenders of democracy against fascism. In France they were part of the Popular Front. In the United States they supported Roosevelt and the New Deal. In Spain they fought against Franco side by side with men who believed in democracy, although the communists later betrayed the Spanish democrats.

Three ideologies competed for control of the world. And, as events turned out, one totalitarian nation—the Soviet Union—would finally be forced to stand with the democracies against the totalitarians of Germany, Italy, and Japan in the most terrible war in the history of the world.

MUSSOLINI MEETS WITH HITLER AND GOERING IN GERMANY.

SOLDIERS STAND AT ATTENTION AT A NAZI MASS MEETING.

IMPORTANT EVENTS – TOTALITARIANISM

1926 English trade unions call a general strike but are forced to return to work after nine days.
1928 Stalin exiles Trotsky and consolidates his power, beginning the first Five Year Plan to industrialize Russia; Mussolini's new constitution makes Italy a fascist dictatorship.
1929 The stock market crash marks beginning of Depression in U. S.
1931 Spain becomes a republic when King Alfonso flees; Japanese troops invade Manchuria, causing war with China.
1932 The "Bonus Army" marches on Washington and is dispersed by troops under General MacArthur.
1933 Roosevelt becomes president and takes steps to solve the financial crisis in America; Hitler is made chancellor of Germany and uses the Reichstag fire as an excuse to suppress communists and others; the Reichstag grants him dictatorial powers.
1934 Fascist riots in Paris follow the Stavisky scandal; Hitler wipes out opponents in the Nazi party in the "Blood Purge."

The Museum of Modern Art, N. Y.

AND THE DEPRESSION, 1926-1938

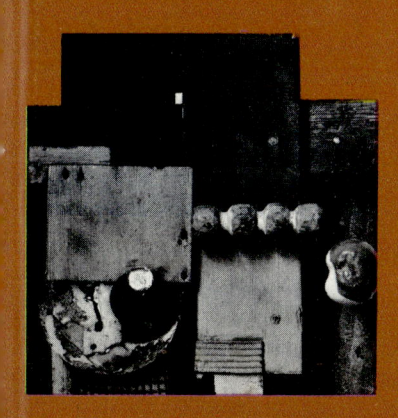

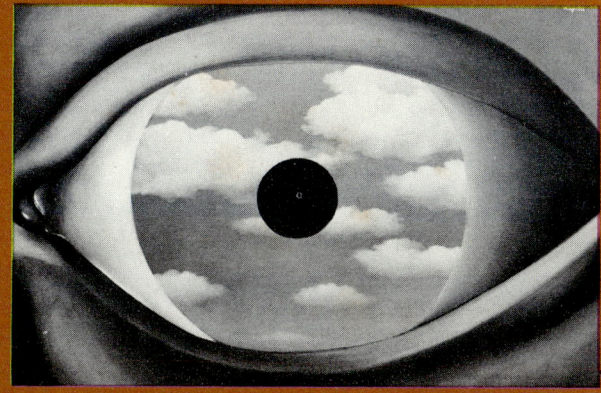

The Museum of Modern Art, N.Y.

1935 The U.S. Supreme Court declares the NRA unconstitutional; Italy invades Ethiopia.
1936 Spanish fascists led by General Franco revolt against the republic, starting the Civil War; Stalin wipes out the Old Bolsheviks in the Moscow purge trials; Roosevelt is re-elected by a huge margin; a Popular Front government is elected in France and begins sweeping reforms; fascist Italy completes its conquest of Ethiopia and joins Germany in supporting Franco in Spain.
1937 Roosevelt's attempt to enlarge the Supreme Court fails; Nazi Germany tests new methods of warfare in Spain, bombing the town of Guernica from the air; the French government frustrates plans for a fascist coup.
1938 Jews are arrested and murdered and their homes burned during the "Week of Broken Glass" in Germany; the French Popular Front collapses and the new government reverses many of the reforms it had enacted; the world moves rapidly toward a new world war.

The Museum of Modern Art, N.Y.